# THE
# GREEN MOUNTAIN
# BOYS OF
# HENRI-CHAPELLE

## STORIES OF VERMONT'S WWII SOLDIERS

# AIMEE GAGNON FOGG

*For Them*

*For Those Who Loved Them*

*For Those Who Mourn Them*

U.S. MILITARY CEMETERY, HENRI-CHAPELLE, BELGIUM

(Photo courtesy of Superintendent Bobby Bell.)

*"There lies a hill just east of Flanders,*
*    where Doughboys lie who fought so well.*
*And there they sleep beneath the crosses,*
*    while softly chimes a chapel bell.*
*Winds that blow o'er lives undaunted,*
*    respect the thousands strong who fell.*
*And morning dawn arise in silence,*
*    awake them not for all is well.*
*We who live must long remember,*
*    and seek the peace where brave men dwell.*
*Could we but hear them ask the question,*
*    is this the last Henri-Chapelle?*
*The Hill of Henri-Chapelle,*
*    where the free and the brave men dwell.*
*And helpless hands place rows of roses,*
*    where the free and the brave men dwell,*
*On the Hill of Henri-Chapelle."*

(Photo courtesy of Author.)

"As Superintendent of these hallowed grounds, it's an honor to maintain the final resting place of those who died young so that we may grow old in peace and prosperity."

~ Bobby Bell, Superintendent of Henri-Chapelle Cemetery

(Photo courtesy of Author.)

# STAR-SPANGLED BANNER

*O say can you see by the dawn's early light,*
*What so proudly we hailed at the twilight's last gleaming,*
*Whose broad stripes and bright stars through the perilous fight,*
*O'er the ramparts we watched, were so gallantly streaming?*
*And the rockets' red glare, the bombs bursting in air,*
*Gave proof through the night that our flag was still there;*
*O say does that star-spangled banner yet wave,*
*O'er the land of the free and the home of the brave?*

*On the shore dimly seen through the mists of the deep,*
*Where the foe's haughty host in dread silence reposes,*
*What is that which the breeze, o'er the towering steep,*
*As it fitfully blows, half conceals, half discloses?*
*Now it catches the gleam of the morning's first beam,*
*In full glory reflected now shines in the stream:*
*Tis the star-spangled banner, O! long may it wave*
*O'er the land of the free and the home of the brave.*

*And where is that band who so vauntingly swore*
*That the havoc of war and the battle's confusion,*
*A home and a country, should leave us no more?*
*Their blood has washed out their foul footsteps' pollution.*
*No refuge could save the hireling and slave*
*From the terror of flight, or the gloom of the grave:*
*And the star-spangled banner in triumph doth wave,*
*O'er the land of the free and the home of the brave.*

*O thus be it ever, when freemen shall stand*
*Between their loved home and the war's desolation.*
*Blest with vict'ry and peace, may the Heav'n rescued land*
*Praise the Power that hath made and preserved us a nation!*
*Then conquer we must, when our cause it is just,*
*And this be our motto: "In God is our trust."*
*And the star-spangled banner in triumph shall wave*
*O'er the land of the free and the home of the brave!*

*~ Francis Scott Key*

# TABLE OF CONTENTS

# AUTHOR'S NOTE

I did not plan to research the Vermont soldiers interred at Henri-Chapelle American Cemetery in Homburg, Belgium. I did not plan to research the New Hampshire soldiers interred there as well, for that matter, or publish those stories in *The Granite Men of Henri-Chapelle*. I simply planned on researching my great-uncle, PFC Paul M. Lavoie of Nashua, New Hampshire, KIA February 10, 1945, in Germany, to find his burial location. I also did not plan on traveling his route of march through Europe, visiting Henri-Chapelle, or meeting the Belgian couple, Jacques and Ann Marie Cormann, who adopted his cross and visit on a frequent basis. That was back in 2010 and many people, their stories, and miles ago.

The 57-acre World War Two cemetery impacted me. The 7,992 white marble markers beckoned me for a closer look. The men and their stories called. I decided to answer.

These stories of Vermont's twenty-five men are a celebration of life, a recognition of lives lived, and an acknowledgment of those who answered the call of duty and did not return to their families, communities, or futures.

May those who have fallen in service to their country always be remembered and respected.

# DEATH IS NOTHING AT ALL

*Death is nothing at all*
*I have only slipped away into the next room*
*I am I and you are you*
*Whatever we were to each other*
*That we are still*
*Call me by my old familiar name*
*Speak to me in the easy way you always used*
*Put no difference into your tone*
*Wear no forced air of solemnity or sorrow*
*Laugh as we always laughed*
*At the little jokes we always enjoyed together*
*Play, smile, think of me, pray for me*
*Let my name be ever the household word that it always was*
*Let it be spoken without effort*
*Without the ghost of a shadow in it*

*Life means all that it ever meant*
*It is the same as it ever was*
*There is absolute unbroken continuity*
*What is death but a negligible accident?*
*Why should I be out of mind*
*Because I am out of sight?*
*I am waiting for you for an interval*
*Somewhere very near*
*Just around the corner*

*All is well.*
*Nothing is past; nothing is lost*
*One brief moment and all will be as it was before*
*How we shall laugh at the trouble of parting when we meet again!*

*~ Canon Henry Scott-Holland, 1847-1918*

# ACKNOWLEDGMENTS

I wish to extend much appreciation and gratitude to the following individuals at various Vermont historical societies and libraries for all of their research assistance: Mary Ayer, Sharon Historical Society; Judy Brown, Norwich Historical Society; Lois Frey, Johnson Historical Society; and Kathy Tulissi, Grand Isle Public Library.

These stories also would not have been possible without the dedicated assistance of Vance Asselin at Vermont Department of Libraries. Thank you again.

I also wish to thank Jason Starr of *Essex Reporter* and Scott Wheeler of *Vermont's Northland Journal* for publishing stories about this project.

Many thanks and appreciative gratitude to the families and friends of these soldiers who answered my initial letter or phone call and who welcomed me into their homes and into their lives. Thank you for granting me the opportunity to get to know your relatives and to write their stories. I truly enjoyed talking with each of you and sharing this experience together. My life has been enriched. They are: Rosalee Bills and Neil Humphrey, daughter and grandson of PFC Louis Connolly; Cecilia Baker Bressette and Debbie Baker, sister and niece of Pvt. Leroy Baker; Barbara Chapin, niece of PFC Claude Chapin; Jackie Durkee, sister-in-law of PVT James Durkee; Shirley Holt &and Catherine McKenney, sisters of PFC Garth Whittier; Lynn and David Gauthier and their Gauthier cousins, cousins of PVT Albert Gauthier; Natalie Gruber, sister of PVT Logan Warner; Arthur Jacobs and Florence Joyal, nephew and niece of SSGT Arthur Jacobs; George Joyal and Debra Viens, nephew and niece of PVT Adelard Joyal and SSGT George Joyal; Dolores Luebke, cousin of SGT Edward Jones, Jr.; Harold Mitchell Jr., son of PFC Harold Mitchell; Norine Royer and Bev Hall, sister and niece of PVT Lawrence Bishop and SGT Norman Bishop; Jerry Schuebel, nephew of PFC Howard Lapan; Peter Rogers, brother of PFC Royal Rogers.

Thank you to Donna Builder for help collecting information for PFC Theodore Hall's story, to Robert Guerin for writing PVT Gerard Desroches' personal history, and to researcher Patti Johnson for sharing CAPT Richard Prentiss' material with me.

Thank you to Tom Peeters, who referred me to Glen Stimets, who led me to Helen Siple, sister of PVT Thomas Sorrell, and James Sorrell, nephew of PVT Sorrell. I really enjoyed working with Glen, Helen, and James on PVT Sorrell's story and believe our collaborative efforts would please him.

Thank you to Robert Tomlinson, son-in-law of CPL Maurice Metivier. Your help honors the lives of both your late wife, Wanda, and her father. Thank you to Gerry Eggleston as well.

Thank you to Jeannine Young for your editing services and assistance.

Thank you to Roger and Joanne Gagnon of Irasburg, Vermont, for participating in this adventure and for welcoming us into your home! Thank you for your service in Vietnam, Roger.

Thank you to Commander Jim Harlow with American Legion Lyman Pell Post #8 for allowing me to use the Norwich facility during closed hours to interview PVT James Durkee's family. Appreciated the warm building on that very cold January day!

Thank you as well to Hattie Duncan for your expertise and kindness.

Thank you to Superintendent Bobby Bell, Assistant Superintendent Lou Aske, and to the personnel at Henri-Chapelle. Much gratitude to them as well for making certain the cemetery remains a sacred resting place for thousands of American soldiers.

I would like to especially thank my parents, Ronald and Margaret Gagnon, for teaching me to dream big and aim high in life, and to my husband as well as best friend, Ryan, for continuously supporting me not only with this project, but with all my special endeavors. Your encouragement as well as help is much appreciated, needed, and valued. To Isabella, Chapelle, and Robert Paul: remember who you are and your limitless potential. Never accept no for an answer when leaving your footprints on this world.

Last, a thank you to the 7,992 men who permanently rest at Henri-Chapelle American Cemetery.

(Photo courtesy of Author.)

# INTRODUCTION

Fort Ticonderoga stood before them in the early morning of May 10, 1775. They waited as their leader, Ethan Allen, surveyed the British-controlled fort before launching their surprise attack.[1] They were bold. They were courageous. They were successful. These men, who had come together in the early American Revolutionary years to keep New York settlers out of Vermont, wanted freedom.[2] These men, considered to be the founding fathers of Vermont, fought hard for that independence. They knew their objective. They knew their enemy. They knew their role in the creation of their country. They were the Green Mountain Boys.

World War Two impacted nearly every American home either directly or indirectly. Men marched off to war. Many would not return. Women entered the work force. Children learned the meanings of ration stamps, victory gardens, and blackouts. Telegrams from the War Department informing families of their relatives' fate became a sad reality and norm. Citizens entered the military to serve their country and to do their part in protecting freedom. Due to the high number of personnel who entered the Army, serial numbers were given to each individual to prevent confusion. According to a report issued by the War Department on January 31, 1946:

> Regular Army enlisted men who entered the service before the onset of Selective Service bear seven-digit or lower serial numbers, usually beginning with "6" or "7" . . . Men who enlisted in the Army of the United States have eight-digit numbers beginning with "1," the second digit indicating the Service Command of origin . . . Men called into federally recognized National Guard service received eight-digit numbers beginning with "2," the third digit representing

the Service Command. Men inducted or enlisted through Selective Service were given eight-digit numbers beginning with "3" or "4," the second digit representing the Service Command. The prefixed serial numbers for other than male enlisted personnel carry a designated letter: O- (as is O-1574257) for male commissioned officers; W- for male Warrant officers, T- for Flight officers of the Army Air Forces; L- for commissioned officers of the Women's Army Corp; V- for WAC Warrant officers; A- for WAC enlisted women; R- for Hospital Dietitians, and M- for Physical Therapy Aides.[3]

The report further explains that of the men and women of Vermont who went to war, 3.57 percent failed to return.[4]

Twenty-five of these Vermont soldiers who failed to return rest at Henri-Chapelle American Cemetery in Homburg, Belgium, between Liège and Aachen, Germany. This cemetery is the final resting place for 7,992 American soldiers from forty-seven other states, from the District of Columbia, and from Panama as well as England. There are thirty-three instances of two brothers buried next to one another in addition to one instance of three brothers resting side by side. There are also tombs of ninety-four unknown soldiers.[5] The service members interred at Henri-Chapelle were killed during the Huertgen-Forest campaign, the Battle of the Bulge, and the Allied advance into Germany. Others perished in air operations over the region.[6] Furthermore, the names of 450 Missing in Action soldiers, including one from Vermont, are also inscribed on the Tablets of the Missing colonnade area at the cemetery's front entrance. American soldiers with the 1st Infantry Division liberated the region in early September 1944, and established a temporary cemetery by the end of the month.[7]

By the end of the war, the United States Army had established several hundred temporary cemeteries on battlefields around the world. Henri-Chapelle was the largest temporary American cemetery in Europe with over 17,000 soldiers interred there.[8] Public Law 368, passed by the 80th Congress in 1947, allowed authorized next of kin to select one of three options for permanent disposition of a loved one's remains. The alternatives were permanent interment in an American military cemetery on foreign soil, repatriation to America for interment in a private cemetery, or repatriation to America for interment in a national cemetery.[9] Final disposition of remains became the responsibility of the War Department's American Graves Registration Service under the Quartermaster General. The repatriation program began in July of 1947 with more than half of the 17,000 soldiers at Henri-Chapelle repatriated to America for burial.[10] The completion of Henri-Chapelle as a permanent American military cemetery occurred in 1960 and today is regulated by the American Battle Monuments Commission. From the American Battle Monuments Commission:

> Established by Congress in 1923, the American Battle Monuments Commission (ABMC) commemorates the service, achievements, and sacrifice of U.S. armed forces. ABMC manages 24 overseas military cemeteries, and 25 memorials, monuments, and markers. Nearly all the cemeteries and memorials specifically honor those who served in World War I or World War II.
>
> The sacrifice of more than 218,000 U.S. servicemen and women is memorialized at these locations. Nearly 125,000 American war dead are buried at ABMC cemeteries, with an additional 94,000 individuals commemorated on Tablets of the Missing.[11]

The personal histories contained in this book are not war stories. Rather, they are an attempt to illustrate each civilian life before the war, as well as to capture the person behind the military rank. For this reason, I decided not to include the cause of death for each man. In addition to relying on genealogy tools, historical societies, and family members, if located and available, I also used Enlistment Records and requested Individual Deceased Personnel Files from the Army for all twenty-five men. Individual Deceased Personnel

Files were generated when a soldier died, and contain documents that detail what happened to the body from the time the soldier was killed until his permanent burial. Each soldier's IDPF also contains correspondence between family and the military, medal citations, and an Army Effects Bureau report. Some IDPFs contain many documents, whereas others contain just a few pages of information. Certain stories are longer and more complete than others. In some instances, I was simply unable to locate any relatives, comrades, or community members who remembered these men or who wanted to help. The St. Louis fire, which destroyed 80% of WWII records, along with the passage of more than seventy years, essentially became my biggest obstacle in researching and collecting each story. Although various research obstacles presented themselves, I was still able to find enough information to write at least one page for each man.

In the words of Vermont native and America's 30th President, John Calvin Coolidge Jr., "No person was ever honored for what he received. Honor has been the reward for what he gave." They gave their all, the Green Mountain Boys of Henri-Chapelle.

(Photo courtesy of Author.)

# PRIVATE
# LEROY L. BAKER

*87ᵗʰ Armored Field Artillery Battalion Battery B*
*KIA March 8, 1945*
*Medals: Purple Heart*
*Serial #11008805*
*Plot C Row 4 Grave 32*

Leroy Lester Baker was born on August 22, 1923, to George and Irene (Decoigne) of Pownal, Vermont.[1] He joined a sister, Ida, along with a brother, Elmer.[2] Brother Kenneth arrived in March 1927, and died one month later from accidental smothering in bed.[3] By 1930, the Baker family had expanded, with the arrival of four-year-old Lillian and one-year-old Cecilia.[4] The family continued to grow during the 1930s with the addition of two more daughters, Charlotte and Jean, along with two more sons, Bernard and George.[5]

(Photo courtesy of
Cecilia Baker Bressette.)

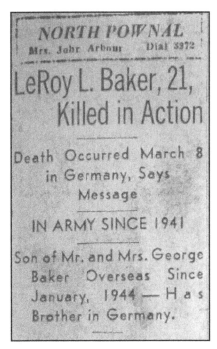

Sister Cecilia Baker Bressette contends her brothers each had unique nicknames. Leroy was no different. He was known as "Jack" and the family today still references him as such. Although a six-year age difference existed between Cecilia and Jack, the older brother treated his younger sister with a warm love that she can still feel, as evidenced by the look in her eyes as she gazes at his photos. Her favorite memory of him is how he taught her to ice skate on the pond behind their home. She didn't have any ice skates and Jack let her use his very large pair. He was her compassionate and loving brother, who "would have been a good dad because he loved kids."[6]

When he wasn't hunting, fishing, or trapping animals with his oldest brother, Elmer, Jack liked to play baseball. In fact, the New York Yankees wanted to draft his father, George, in 1929. The desires of the Yankees were no match for the desires of a wife and mother who said no. The Baker family did not own a car and everyone just simply walked to his or her destination. Cecilia believes this is maybe why Jack completed only two years of high school since the school itself was located an inconvenient distance from their home. He also worked in the manufacture of leather.[7]

Eight days after his 18th birthday, Leroy joined the military on August 30, 1941. Brother Elmer had joined on September 9, 1940. Cecilia wrote letters to her two brothers every day. Jack, being the kind of brother he was, always responded. "He had beautiful penmanship," remembers Cecilia, "especially for someone who wrote with his left hand."[8] After training at Fort Devens, South Carolina, and at Fort Bragg in North Carolina, Jack was then assigned to Fort

Clayton and Fort William Davis in the Canal Zone. He served more than two years in the Canal Zone and it was from there that he wrote his sister, Lillian, the following letter, dated May 9, 1942:

My dearest sister Lillian,
  I received your loving letter today and was very glad to hear from you. I am very glad to hear that you got a raise and I am very grateful for you asking me if I wanted anything. And I appreciate you getting me a wristwatch. You don't have to worry about me not answering your letters because I will answer every one you send me and will be very glad you think so much of me. I will be looking forward of receiving that old picture of you. I will have it enlarged and keep it in my locker. You don't want to feel bad because I am away from home because I am here for a good cause. And when I get home I hope I can make you all feel proud of me that I had a chance like this to fight for what we all want most. Don't think of what happened in the past, just think of what it is going to be like in the future. You told me to ask ( ) to write, but I can't because I never see him anymore because ( ) different places. So I hope you understand. The last letter I wrote Ma I told her I was sending a picture of me and some of the fellows but I forgot to put it in the letter so I am putting it in this letter I am sending her. Kiss little George for me and the other kids and Ma and Dad. Who is the girl friend you chum around with now? Have her drop me a line if she

(Photo courtesy of Cecilia Baker Bressette.)

will. Well, I'll have to close now hoping to hear from you soon. Don't forget to answer me. From your loving brother,

"Jack" Love & Kisses[9]

Private Baker eventually returned to the United States where he was assigned to Fort Knox, Kentucky. There he took up boxing and earned the nickname "Punchey". Leroy, the boy from Pownal, had developed into "Punchey", a Golden Glove winner. He also had his heart captured by a girl named Vivian Brown during this time and mailed Cecilia a photo of her. Private Baker deployed overseas to England with the 87th Armored Field Artillery Battalion in January of 1944, where he participated in further training exercises and preparation for D-Day.[10]

Private Baker, who had a tattoo on his right arm, went ashore on Utah Beach on June 8, 1944, and fought his way through Western Europe.[11] In March of 1945, Private Baker found himself engaging the enemy on the banks of the Rhine River in Germany. The older brother, who had entered the military a year before Jack, found himself providing reinforcements to his younger brother. The two brothers who had spent so much time together in the Green Mountains of Vermont were together again, only this time under different circumstances. Cecilia states that Elmer went to Jack's commanding officer, requesting to see his younger brother. The officer granted the request. Elmer was able to confirm that Jack had indeed provided his ultimate sacrifice. He never spoke about the details of what he saw, according to Cecilia. Nine months after arriving on Utah Beach, Private Baker was killed in action on March 8, 1945, while crossing the Rhine River.[12] A bottle of perfume, a German cap, a pocket watch, a wrist watch, and a camera were items among his personal effects.[13]

Jack came home on two leaves and his family was very happy to have him back, even for a short time. He knew he would not survive the war and expressed his final wishes to his parents during his last visit home. Private Baker requested to be buried where he fought for his country, and although the family knew of his premonition, his death devastated them all, especially fifteen-year-old Cecilia. She said her heart broke when the family finally received the War Department telegram. Jack's death broke the heart of another female: that of his mother. Cecilia remembers her mother crying often, especially at night when she thought no one could hear her.[14]

"He was a good person who loved life, his country, and the military. He was very proud of his service," states Cecilia.[15] In a letter to his sister Lillian, Private Baker expresses a desire to make his family all feel proud of him upon his return home. He may not have returned to Pownal, Vermont, yet his family, especially Cecilia, couldn't be prouder of him.

(Photo courtesy of Cecilia Baker Bressette.)

---

*"Our Flag does not fly
Because the wind moves it.
It flies with the last breath
Of each soldier who died protecting it."*

*~ Unknown*

---

# SERGEANT NORMAN E. BISHOP

# PRIVATE LAWRENCE H. BISHOP

*315th Infantry, 79th Division*

*KIA December 14, 1944*
*Medals: Purple Heart,*
*          Oak Leaf Cluster*
*Serial #31340481*
*Plot H Row 15 Grave 59*

*504th Parachute Infantry,*
*82nd Airborne Division*
*KIA December 21, 1944*
*Medals: Purple Heart*

*Serial #31403465*
*Plot H Row 15 Grave 58*

The 11th hour of the 11th day of the 11th month of 1918 formally ended World War One with the German signing of the Armistice. For young Norman Edward Bishop of Derby, Vermont, November 11, 1918, marked his fourth birthday celebration with parents, Henry and Norabella (Dresser), as well as with two older sisters and one younger sister.[1] Norman was his parents' third child and first son. His two older sisters, Beatrice and Lillian, were both born in Canada prior to the family's move to America, specifically to a town located in Vermont's Northeast Kingdom region.[2] Norman was born in Holland, Vermont.[3] By the 1920 census, the family, which included Beatrice, Lillian, Norman, Alice, and Henrietta, resided

Lawrence H. Bishop

Norman E. Bishop

(Photo courtesy of Norine Bishop Royer.)

(Photo courtesy of Norine Bishop Royer.)

in Orleans, Vermont.[4] An eight-year-old Norman finally gained a brother in 1921 with the arrival of Lawrence Henry on August 19. A sister whom Henry and Norabella named Norine greeted her older siblings in 1927. Norman became his parents' eldest son when they welcomed their eighth and last child in 1934. They named him Kenneth.[5]

Both Norman and Lawrence completed grammar school in Holland, Vermont, and the two brothers followed in their parents' footsteps, becoming farmers.[6] According to the 1940 census, Lawrence, nicknamed "Pete", worked as a laborer and lived at the residence belonging to Milton K. Willey of Derby, Vermont.[7] In fact, Norman and Lawrence's niece, Bev Hall, states that Lawrence "Pete" started working on the Willey farm in April 1935 as a thirteen-year-old boy. Norman and Lawrence were both hard working individuals. Lawrence at times worked eighty-four hours a week at the Willey farm.[8]

Youngest sister Norine Bishop Royer remembers her two older brothers enjoyed fishing and playing baseball. Norman, who did not have any nickname, was known to have a temper at appropriate times and could get things done. He was also considered an extrovert. Lawrence, on the other hand, was mellower, easy-going, and introverted. Neither Norman nor Lawrence married or had any children. Norine fondly remembers her two brothers as overall great individuals who worked hard and who loved their family.[9]

If the Bishop family could be described in one word, it would be tenacious. Norman and Lawrence's father, Henry, died from cancer on April 1, 1942, at the age of 53.[10] Less than two years after his father's death, Lawrence entered the military on December 21, 1943.[11] Assigned to the 504th Parachute Infantry of the 82nd Airborne Division, Lawrence was shot over Belgium and died from his wounds on December 21, 1944, at Cider Red aid station in Belgium a year after entering the military. He was initially known as Unknown X-252 until proper identification could be determined.[12] Norman entered the military in August 1943 and served with the 315th Infantry of the 79th Division. He was killed in action on December 14, 1944, in the vicinity of Marienthal, France, a week before Lawrence's death and was temporarily interred at the United States Military Cemetery in Hochfelden, France.[13] Bishop Royer remembers being told that Norman had been shot in the face and had the option of coming home. He declined, as he did not want his mother to see him.[14]

As Norabella ate Christmas dinner with her daughter Norine, her son Kenneth, and a friend, she received notification of her son Norman's death. A short time later, in the presence of Norine and Kenneth once again, Norabella received notification of Lawrence's death. Norine Bishop Royer states that her mother was absolutely devastated by her sons' deaths and never really was the same again. Her spirit seemed to be broken. Norabella remained a widow and never really spoke about Norman or Lawrence. The family ultimately decided to have the two brothers permanently interred side by side at Henri-Chapelle in 1949.[15]

The *Newport Daily Express* published the brothers' combined death notice on January 25, 1945:

Sgt. Norman Bishop and Pvt. Lawrence Bishop were killed in action on the western front. Sons of Mrs. Norabella Bishop of 17 Bay Street, Newport, the two Newport young men were reported killed within a week of each other. Norman fell in action on December 14 in France and Lawrence died December 21 as a result of wounds received in Belgium.

The young men were born in the town of Holland. Both attended the Holland public schools and Lawrence was a pupil for a time in the Bates school in the town of Derby and the East school in Newport city.

Norman, the first to enter the Army, left Newport in August, 1943. He trained at Camp Gruber, Okla., and Camp Phillips, Salina, Kans. He went overseas with an infantry unit on April 29, 1944.

Lawrence signed up with the Army paratroopers on January 11, 1943; training at Camp Blanding, Fla; Fort Benning, Ga; and going overseas from Fort Meade, Md., in late September of 1944.

The War Department has expressed sympathy to Mrs. Bishop in the loss of her two fine sons and assures her that both died heroically and courageously in the line of duty.

"Through your sorrow we hope you will understand our pride in their heroism and devotion to duty," the War Department spokesman wrote Mrs. Bishop.[16]

Norabella Bishop wrote the following letter to the Quartermaster General's Office dated July 7, 1945:

I am writing in answer to the letter regarding my son Sergeant Norman E. Bishop's effects.

No my son was not married. He was my whole dependence. His father is also dead for 3 years. My son took care of myself,

UEP 52P/25 COLLECT 4 EXTRA

RIDGEFIELD CONN FEB 5 1949 1010A

VOGL MEMORIAL DIVISION

OQMG 0116659Z WASHDC


MY DESIRE IS TO HAVE MY BROTHERS LEFT BURIED OVER THERE.

THEIR NAMES ARE NORMAN E BISHOP   LAWRENCE H BISHOP

MRS BEATRICE BISHOP KELLEY    PROSPECT STREET   RIDGEFIELD CONN

1146A

---

☑ 1. BE INTERRED IN A PERMANENT AMERICAN MILITARY CEMETERY OVERSEAS. HENRI-CHAPELLE, BELGIUM.

☐ 2. BE RETURNED TO THE UNITED STATES OR ANY POSSESSION OR TERRITORY THEREOF FOR INTERMENT BY NEXT OF KIN IN A PRIVATE CEMETERY

_____
(NAME AND LOCATION OF CEMETERY)

☐ 3. BE RETURNED TO _____, THE HOMELAND OF THE DECEASED OR NEXT OF KIN FOR INTERMENT BY NEXT OF KIN IN A
(FOREIGN COUNTRY)

PRIVATE CEMETERY LOCATED AT_____
(LOCATION OF CEMETERY SELECTED)

☐ 4. BE RETURNED TO THE UNITED STATES FOR FINAL INTERMENT IN A NATIONAL CEMETERY LOCATED AT _____(LOCATION OF NATIONAL CEMETERY SELECTED)

(Please indicate if your own religious services at a location other than the selected national cemetery are desired by placing an "X" in the proper box)

☐ YES    ☐ NO

THE NAME OF THE DECEASED, THE SERIAL NUMBER AND GRADE ARE CORRECT EXCEPT FOR THE FOLLOWING CHANGES: (If no corrections are necessary, indicate this fact by inserting the word "NONE" in the space below.)

*None*

FOR SIDE BY SIDE INTERMENT IN HENRI-CHAPELLE CEMETERY WITH BROTHER:,

Pvt LAWRENCE H. BISHOP, 31 403 465, HENRI-CHAPELLE, BELGIUM, OO-3-58

OQMG FORM 345 MILITARY    FEB 8 1949    PAGE 1

16-60411-1

---

Reference is made to your "RDR" form pertaining to the ///////////////
final interment of the remains of your brothers, the late_____and
_____.

I am gratified to inform you that in accordance with your expressed
  desire, the remains of your brothers will rest overseas in adjoining
grave sites in a permanent American Military Cemetery.

All necessary arrangements for burial, military honors and religious
  services will be completed and provided by the Government. When final
interment has been accomplished, you will be informed of the exact
location/within the cemetery, and the flag used to drape the caskets
    of their graves
during interment services will be forwarded to you.

My deepest sympathy is extended to you in your great loss, and if we
can assist you further, do not hesitate to communicate with us at your
convenience.

2 CC:

Mother Norabella and sister Norine.

(Photo courtesy of Norine Bishop Royer.)

mother Norabella Bishop, and my only other little son left, Kenneth, 11yrs.

Sgt. Norman Bishop had no will of any kind. No one else to look after other than his mother. I think I would like the things and photos as he had those things close to him for keeps probably from home. Nothing can make me feel any worse for my two sons lost over there both in December. I look forward to have them back.

I would appreciate it if the things were sent very much. I will thank you very much in this letter.

Sincerely,

(Mother of a lovely boy)

Mrs. Norabella Bishop[17]

Although Norman's thoughts and emotions regarding his younger brother's entrance into the military will never be known, what is evident is their close relationship. Although Norine Bishop Royer is sad she lost two brothers, she is extremely proud of them both for fighting for freedom, for serving their country, and for helping their fellow man. She finds comfort in the fact that they are buried next to one another in a land they fought to liberate. Norine's oldest son, Lawrence, followed in his uncles' paths and served in the military. Like them, he traveled to a far-away land wearing his country's uniform.[18] Unlike them, though, he returned home.

---

*"In the beginning of a change, the patriot is*
*a scarce man, and brave, and hated and scorned.*
*When his cause succeeds, the timid join him,*
*for then it costs nothing to be a patriot."*

*~ Mark Twain*

---

# PRIVATE FIRST CLASS
# JOHN E. CARLETON

*346th Infantry Regiment, 87th Infantry Division*
*KIA March 4, 1945*
*Medals: Purple Heart*
*Serial # 31404114*
*Plot H Row 1 Grave 22*

John Elijah was born on November 4, 1922, to Frank and Lucy (Holden) Carleton in Windham, Vermont.[1] John was the couple's sixth child out of nine children.[2] The family later moved to Proctor, Vermont, where John completed grammar school.[3] He also worked for the Vermont Marble Company[4], the same company that contributed marble to Arlington National Cemetery, *U.S.S. Arizona* Memorial, and Washington Monument among other places.[5]

Twenty-one-year-old John Carleton entered the military on August 29, 1944, as a single man with no dependents.[6] He

(Photo courtesy of
*Rutland Daily Herald.*)

Pfc John E. Carleton, 31 404 114
Plot E, Row 4, Grave 94,
United States Military Cemetery
Foy, Belgium

5 January 1948

Mr. Frank E. Carleton
28 Green Square
Proctor, Vermont

Dear Mr. Carleton:

The people of the United States, through the Congress have authorized the disinterment and final burial of the heroic dead of World War II. The Quartermaster General of the Army has been entrusted with this sacred responsibility to the honored dead. The records of the War Department indicate that you may be the nearest relative of the above-named deceased, who gave his life in the service of his country.

The enclosed pamphlets, "Disposition of World War II Armed Forces Dead," and "American Cemeteries," explain the disposition, options and services made available to you by your Government. If you are the next of kin according to the line of kinship as set forth in the enclosed pamphlet, "Disposition of World War II Armed Forces Dead," you are invited to express your wishes as to the disposition of the remains of the deceased by completing Part I of the enclosed form "Request for Disposition of Remains." Should you desire to relinquish your rights to the next in line of kinship, please complete Part II of the enclosed form. If you are not the next of kin, please complete Part III of the enclosed form.

If you should elect Option 2, it is advised that no funeral arrangements or other personal arrangements be made until you are further notified by this office.

Will you please complete the enclosed form, "Request for Disposition of Remains" and mail in the enclosed self-addressed envelope, which requires no postage, within 30 days after its receipt by you? Its prompt return will avoid unnecessary delays.

Sincerely,

THOMAS B. LARKIN
Major General
The Quartermaster General

4 Incls.

chb

served with the 346[7] Infantry Regiment of the 87[7] Infantry Division and was initially classified as missing in action on February 12, 1945, in Germany.[7] His parents received further notification that their son's status had changed status from missing in action on February 12, 1945, to missing in action on March 4, 1945, in Germany. They finally received notification that their son had been declared killed in action on March 4, 1945, in Germany.[8]

---

*"To the Memory of the Gallant Men Here Entombed and their shipmates who gave their lives in action on December 7, 1941, on the* **U.S.S. Arizona.** *"*

~ **U.S.S. Arizona** *Memorial*

---

# PRIVATE FIRST CLASS
# CLAUDE B. CHAPIN

*550th Airborne Infantry Battalion*
*KIA January 4, 1945*
*Medals: Purple Heart*
*Serial # 31062373*
*Plot E Row 13 Grave 20*

In the 1860s, a man named Albert Chapin bought a farm in Essex, Vermont. In the early 1870s, he bought additional land and built a house and barn on the property. He continued to farm the 300 or so acres until his death in 1888.[1] His great-grandson Claude Buell Chapin was born on August 3, 1914, at the Chapin family homestead in Essex. A midwife delivered Claude and Clara (Brand) Chapin's fourth child and second son in the

(Photo courtesy of Barbara Chapin.)

only room within the house that contained a door with a window in it.[2] Claude and Clara's first child, a daughter named Dorothy, died in 1912. Their second child and firstborn son, Palmer, died as a baby in 1906. Their third child and second son, named Graton Andrew, welcomed his new brother. 1915 brought another child for Claude and Clara: a son, Lawrence, who died as an infant. The couple welcomed another child and son, James, in

(Photo courtesy of Author.)

1918, who died as a baby from the flu. Graton and Claude gained yet another brother with the birth of William in 1921.[3] Thus, Graton, Claude, and William, the three brothers who survived childhood, were the fourth generation to live on the Chapin farm.

Claude, or "June" as he was called, completed grades one through eight at the Essex Center School. He completed grades nine through twelve at the Essex Classical Institute, graduating in 1932 in a class of five or six other students. He and his older brother, Graton, worked on their father's dairy farm. Their younger brother, William, pursued his own interests. June loved the farming life: making maple syrup, growing corn for the local cannery, maintaining the dairy herd, and raising Morgan horses. He especially loved caring for his apple trees.[4] Niece Barbara Chapin expounds:

> When June was a boy, there was an apple orchard southwest of the house. Apparently, the trees were planted too close together, and in the fall, it was ground to ground apples! In 1929, as the Depression was setting in, June traveled with his dad to the "islands" (South Hero, Grand Isle, North Hero) to purchase apples; they were something like a nickel, dime, or quarter a bushel. Well, June's father thought that was too much, so he and June planted a new orchard of their own, north and west of the house and barn. Today that orchard, along with a newly

*planted one in 1980, brings 10,000 people a season to the original Chapin hay barn. Graton probably preferred managing the dairy herd and making maple syrup, but in June's honor and memory, managed well the orchard until his death in 1982.[5]*

In addition to farming and taking care of his eight-to-ten-acre apple orchard, June also enjoyed hiking the hills around the property and enjoying the views of Lake Champlain, the Green Mountain range, and the Adirondack Mountains from atop these trails. He simply "loved farming life, his family, his beloved hiking hills, and the mountains of Vermont."[6]

Not only did Albert Chapin build and pass on the farm to his posterity, but he also instilled the importance of education as well as sense of duty and service that became synonymous with the Chapin name.[7] Perhaps it was this sense of duty and service to community or perhaps it was the era which June grew up, an era where a man's word was good, an era where neighbors helped neighbors, an era where doors were never locked, that prompted him to voluntarily join the military on February 6, 1942.[8] The farm boy from Vermont, who was known to have a rather serious personality with a high degree of integrity, as well as responsibility, deployed to Europe and

*ra Chapin.)*

CLASS CLAUDE B. CHAPIN ✶ 23

HE

was assigned to the 550[9] Airborne Infantry Battalion. He was killed in action on January 4, 1945, in Bastogne, Belgium.[9] His comrade and friend, Jerome W. Moore, sent the following letter to June's brother, Graton, dated February 18, 1960:

Dear Mr. Chapin,

I received your letter yesterday and have been wondering what I could write in answer to it telling you what happened without adding hurt. I first got to know Claude at Laurinburg–Maxton Army Air Base in North Carolina. We enjoyed many a good long talk. We seemed to have much in common and yet worlds apart in background. I ate some of the maple sugar that was made there on your farm. You probably remember sending the sugar to him. I talked with him of the dairy cattle, the apple orchard, the raising of sweet corn for the cannery, the carrying of the cobs back to use for cow feed.

I'm telling you of this as to identify myself as having known him second only to the family. I even persuaded Claude to go with me to S.C. to see my girlfriend. Perhaps he wrote of this.

Mr. Chapin, if you all understood the feelings that a combat man has in the face of danger, then I'm sure you'd never worry about if we were ready to go, in death, that is. God has a wonderful way of preparing each and every one of us for the task at nd, even to dying. Excuse me, but I have to take time out to y eyes even after 15 years, when I think of this. To be able Be ch and carry on we have to be believe in a Supreme assur de did.

I ho if he could have reached you he would have never ha had no fear of the great unknown.
suffering. A tion will be of some comfort to you. He driving the G that death was near. There was no the Lowlands. k his head off instantly. We were r to cut off their ( ) from out of day – Jan. 4, 1945 and that

RI-CHAPELLE

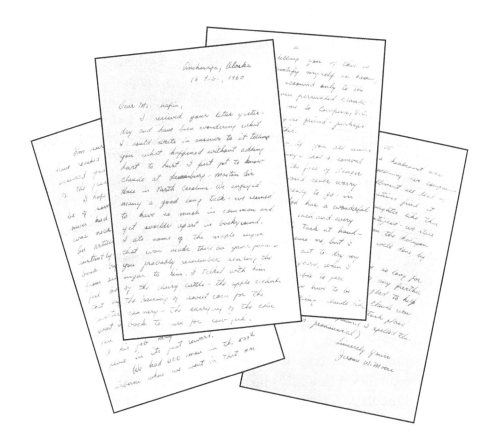

night they staged a savage counterattack and a battle of battles went into ( ). Claude's machine gun was hot from use. He died at his job. May his soul rest in peace in its just reward.

We had 600 men in the 550th Airborne when we went in that AM and 249 when a headcount was taken the next morning. Two companies, B and C, were almost all dead or prisoners. I sometimes find it hard to think slaughter like this has ever been justified. We still have war clouds on the horizon in spite of a job well done by so many.

I'm going to say so long for now. If I can be of any further help to you, I'll be glad to help you. I don't know where Claude was buried over there.[10]

The passing of PFC Claude Chapin devastated his family, yet they remained characteristically stoic. Niece Barbara Chapin explains how Claude's death affected her father, Graton: "The plan had been that the two brothers, Graton and Claude, would be taking over the farm from their father. In the town of Essex, as it turned out, the two largest farms in the '50s and '60s were owned by two brothers. The Chapin farm was the third largest, owned only by Graton. He never complained, but his children feel that his whole life he missed his four-years- younger brother (would-be partner) and had to adjust his dream of how **his** life would unfold."[11]

Although Chapin Orchard is now owned by Phillip and Helen Murdock and co-managed by them along with Jim Bove (and before that managed well by Nick and Bridget Meyer), June's beloved apples are still appreciated by the thousands of visitors who stroll the rows of trees he and his father planted so many years ago. From niece Barbara Chapin: "He never returned to his beloved fields and hills and his dream of sharing the challenge of farming with his brother. He would never have the opportunity to appreciate the fact that people throughout Chittenden County to this day continue to visit

(Photo courtesy of Barbara Chapin.)

and enjoy Chapin Orchard."[12] She continues, "I want him to be remembered for being the genuine, honest, responsible, hard-working, brave man that he was, who loved the land he farmed and the family with whom he farmed, who, although he had a dispensation to avoid going to war (as he was farming), responded to a sense of duty and justice. He enlisted to fight evil and injustice in a faraway land."[13]

(Photo courtesy of Barbara Chapin.)

The main branch running from the trunk of an apple tree straight up through the middle is called a central leader and all other branches grow from this branch. The central leader should also always be the highest branch on a tree. PFC Claude Chapin pruned his beloved apple trees to make certain they would thrive with the fruit of life. They did and continue to do so and although PFC Chapin never returned to his orchard, generations in a distant land thrive with the fruits of freedom secured with the sacrifice of a Vermont farm boy.

---

*"Surely the apple is the noblest of fruits."*

*~ Henry David Thoreau*

---

# PRIVATE FIRST CLASS
# LOUIS V. CONNOLLY

*121ˢᵗ Infantry Regiment, 8ᵗʰ Division*
*KIA February 28, 1945*
*Medals: Purple Heart, Oak Leaf Cluster*
*Serial # 31199790*
*Plot F Row 1 Grave 43*

From grandson Neil Humphrey:

My grandfather, Louis Victor Connolly, was born in Nova Scotia on July 27, 1906. He was thirty-nine years old at the time of his death and was killed at the exact same time as seven other men by an artillery round fired by the Germans at the crossing of the Erft Canal in Germany on 28FEB1945. At the time of their deaths, they were firing artillery rounds at the enemy to protect those making a crossing of the Erft canal near Blatzhiem.

His father, David Connolly, born in Nova Scotia, met and married his second wife, Augusta Como, and had two sons, Louis Victor (who preferred the name Victor), and William Connolly, known to us as "Uncle Bill." They also had two daughters: Edna and Evelyn.

Victor married my grandmother, Ruth Mabel Hescock, and had two daughters: my Aunt Rosalee, the oldest, and Virginia, my mother. Victor first went to school in Montpelier then moved to Rawsonville, Vermont, where his parents ran a farm and country store. He loved motorcycles and was also a featherweight boxer. He loved to box and would work a local circuit to earn money. My Aunt Rosalee had seen him in a couple of matches. He may have been a featherweight boxer in the Army as well.

He landed on the Normandy beaches on July 7, 1944, with the 8th Infantry Division, 121st Infantry, Cannon Company, and fought across France. He was a motorcycle and foot messenger for a time and was wounded in August of 1944 by a gunshot to his right femur. It was while recuperating that he heard of the fighting in the Huertgen Forest. While he did not have to return to the war, he requested to. My Aunt Rosalee questioned this and his reply was that "I have to help my buddies." He was a "cannoneer" with 8th Infantry Division and in the 8th Infantry Division, there is a small note with no names about the eight men killed on February 28, 1945, while crossing the Erft.

On 28FEB1945 my grandfather earned his second Purple Heart...for being killed in action. He was thirty-nine years old at the time of his death and was the oldest among the eight.[1]

The names of the seven other men killed with PFC Connolly are: Tec 5 Annon I. Bozeman Sr., PFC Rex E. Chritchfield, SSGT William N. Cramer, PFC Edward R. Ennis, CPL Harold Roberts, PFC Dymitry Sabot, PVT R.A. White.

Louis was born in Canada, and he and his family immigrated to America circa 1912, settling in the vicinity of Montpelier, Vermont. He loved to read, run, and box. He also possessed beautiful penmanship.[2] After completing grammar school, Louis worked on farms, at lumber mills, and essentially, at any place in need of laborers. Daughter Rosalee Bills remembers her dad as not being afraid to work and doing whatever needed to be done in order to earn a living. She states:

> He worked on several farms in the area, worked on a maple sugaring job in Wardsboro one or two springs, and worked at a lumber saw mill in Jamaica, VT. He also worked at Hale Co. in East Arlington, VT, where beautiful and expensive maple furniture was made. His last job, just before Pearl Harbor, was in Bennington, VT. In the 1930s and '40s, jobs were not always plentiful so everyone worked wherever a job was available.[3]

Prior to entering the military, Louis was always called and known as "Victor" or "Vic". He met his future wife at a dance even though he did not like to dance. He went just to pay lots of attention to a young teenage girl named Ruth Hescock. She was fifteen and he was twenty-two on their July 15, 1929, wedding day in Jamaica, Vermont. As the young couple prepared to celebrate their first wedding anniversary in 1930, they also eagerly waited to meet their first child, a daughter, born on July 23rd. The new father named her Rosalee and she became her daddy's girl from that day forward. "He definitely loved me and I really love him still," states Rosalee. Victor and Ruth welcomed another daughter, Virginia, in 1934, just two years prior to their 1936 divorce. They remained friends after the divorce because of their daughters. Victor also had a good relationship with

(Photo courtesy of Rosalee Connolly Bills.)

Ruth's second husband.[4]

Described as a man with a great sense of humor and a loud belly laugh, but who also possessed a quick temper, Victor could also be described as a man who greatly loved his two daughters. He went to see them on every furlough and did his best to spend as much time with them as possible. Daughter Rosalee states that she had a very close relationship with her father and she "never doubted how much he loved me or my sister." She remembers his visits and how he would have her sit with him, saying, "Get in your old man's lap." During one of his construction jobs, Victor lit lights mornings and

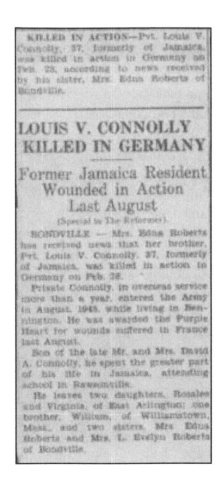

nights at the site. He always carried Rosalee on his shoulders to the site and talked to her as fathers do with their daughters.[5] Early December of 1943 found Rosalee taking yet another walk with her father, this time to bid him farewell for Europe. She walked with him as far as the school and she can still remember noticing how he cried as they walked. She reflects, "It was a very hard parting for overseas." Rosalee, the daughter who saved all fifty-nine letters her father sent her from Europe, made the decision to leave him at Henri-Chapelle Cemetery rather than bring him home to Vermont. She explains, "My father absolutely loved being in the service. He loved his comrades and service to country. He was very patriotic and referred to himself as 'Uncle Sam's Man.'"[6]

She writes in a letter titled *My Dad:*

> PFC Louis Victor Connolly was born in Nova Scotia, Canada, in 1906 and came to the USA when he was seven years old, but never became a citizen until he tried to join the Army right after the attack on Pearl Harbor. As he wasn't an American citizen, he was rejected and came to me, his oldest daughter, to let me know that he was going to Canada to join their Army. Wow! Was I upset! I said, "They bombed us, the USA, not Canada!" I begged him to join our Army so he would be able to visit me on furlough and he did just that! He went for his papers, filled them out, and became a citizen of the US, signed up again, passed all physicals, was accepted, and assigned to the 121$^{st}$ Infantry "Gray Bonnet" regiment, 8$^{th}$ Division ("Golden Arrow"). My first letter from my "Soldier Dad" was from Ft. Devens, MA, in October 1942. (He was sooo proud to be a soldier in the US Army!) He chose the infantry!
>
> The training was rigid: Ft. Leonard Wood, MO, in the cold of winter and Camp Laguna, AZ, for desert training in the heat of summer! (He also trained at Ft. McClellan, AL, and Camp Forrest, TN.)

On December 5th, the outfit sailed from New York Harbor, arriving in Belfast, Ireland, on December 10th, where they received more training until June, 1944. The first wave of the Normandy Invasion was on June 6th and my dad was in the second wave, landing July 4, 1944, on Utah Beach. He fought through France, where he was wounded in the leg, and sent to a hospital in England. His letters from the hospital were: "anxious to get back to the old company and finish the job!" So my dream of him returning home was short-lived. Next letters were written on his way back to his buddies.

So he fought his way through France and in Germany to the Roer River then on through Gieelsrath, Blatzheim, and Kerpen, (almost to the Rhine River) where they were to cross. That was not to be for him because in Kerpen the enemy had zeroed in on the town with "freight cars" rounds, which had a "hell of a swooshing sound" as they moved through the air. Four men were crushed to death as a round struck a building on the first night of the battalion's holding position. Another round hit Cannon Co. and killed 9 men (my dad being one of them!). This was on February 28, 1945, a horrible day!

On March 23, 1945, I received a letter from my dad's brother, Bill, informing me of my dad's death. I was devastated to put it mildly. I was almost 15 years old and was so looking forward to his return home, mostly because the war news was getting much more encouraging and everyone was thinking our guys would be home soon. I knew that "my guy" would not be home! How could I survive that and move on?! I have survived and I eventually moved on, but my one big sadness left is that he didn't get to see me graduate as valedictorian (hope he watched from Heaven!).[7]

PFC Connolly was promoted a month before being killed in action. His death on February 28, 1945, was a tremendous loss for Rosalee. She wrote the following poem in September 1945:

*Something Greater*

*I said, "Oh, Daddy, please don't go to war*
*And leave me here to grow up without you!"*
*You said, "My girl, I'll be back when it's done;*
*There's something greater here than me and you."*

*But, Daddy, you did not come back to me;*
*And though I'm very sure you really tried;*
*I know you were committed to that "cause";*
*And for that "Greater Cause", dear Dad, you died.*

*So I grew up without my Daddy's love;*
*With heartaches always deep within my soul.*
*I felt no joy--just sadness for so long;*
*The lonely years without you took their toll.*

*So, studies, to succeed, and to excel*
*Filled all my lonely hours without you.*
*Though no one else was interested or cared*
*I felt that to your memory I was true.*

*I doubt that you would be real proud of me,*
*For often I gave in to tears and cried*
*(A soldier's daughter should stand straight and tall*
*And keep her tears and sorrows locked inside.)*

*You fell in battle, bloody and alone,*
*Amid war's awful savagery and strife.*
*That "Greater Cause" lives on unto this day*
*Because my Dad, a hero, <u>gave</u> his life.*[8]

She also wrote the following poem dated February 28, 1965:

*My Dad*

*He had a hearty, boisterous laugh*
*That came from deep within;*
*And any little funny joke*
*Would bring a boyish grin.*

*And yet – in contrast – on his face*
*He often wore a frown*
*As though some deep and troubled thought*
*Was there – to weigh him down.*

*Dark eyes that pierced my very soul*
*Yet spoke his love for me;*
*And rough, strong hands – yet gentle*
*As he held me on his knee.*

*And temper! None could match it!*
*(Though he seldom let it show)*
*But when they bombed Pearl Harbor,*
*He really let it go!!*

*He quickly joined the Army*
*His choice? The infantry!!*
*For his intention was to go*
*And fight to keep us free!!*

*His patriotism was unmatched;*
*He had no dread or fears.*
*His country needed good, brave men*
*('Twas I who shed the tears.)*

*I watched him walk away*
*So straight, so tall, so proud was he*
*And I was left alone to weep,*
*With none to comfort me.*

*"Don't cry," he said, "For I'll be back."*
*But "back" he never came*
*I felt so empty, so alone;*
*I can't describe the pain.*

*Life has a way of moving on;*
*And so it was with me.*
*The awful ache has softened some,*
*With years and family.*

*But every now and then the thought*
*Creeps in, (I know it's bad),*
*It wasn't fair for me to have to*
*Give the best I had!!*

*Still, as I look at youth today*
*It's really very sad*
*I see so few that care about*
*This country as did Dad.*

*He bravely marched straight into hell*
*To keep his loved ones free;*
*His medals now are all I have*
*And his proud memory.*

*And when I get to Heaven's gate*
*I pray that I will see*
*Those dark brown eyes and gentle hands*
*Waiting to welcome me.*[9]

Those gentle hands Rosalee prays will welcome her at heaven's gate wrote the following words to his daughter in one of his last letters home:

*Somewhere in Germany*
*January 27, 1945*

Hi 'Tootsie':

*How is my big girl and all the family these cold winter days? I'll bet that there is enough snow to make snow balls and go sliding in over there by now. There is snow over here too, about a foot or 19 inches of it now. Hope that it don't get any deeper. If it does, I'll never find my 'bear den' some dark stormy night and that would be bad, you know.*

*You remember about kidding me about getting back to the "Old 121." Well, I'm back again, have been back almost a month now. It was almost like going home, to get back to the outfit after all the replacement depots that I had to go through.*

*I'm feeling fine and dandy. The old leg healed up fine aside from a nice big scar, I'd never know that I'd been hit.*

*Well, rascal, here goes for some questions. Was 'Old Santa' good to you and Ginnie this Christmas? What do you hear from Uncle Willie & Carol H, how are they making it where they are?*

*I expect that you and Ginnie are making out all right in school. Think that you'll finish grade school this spring? I'll bet you will and next fall it will be high school. Am I right?*

Well, Rosalee, I can't think of any more to write or any more questions to ask. So "bye-bye" for this time.

Love and kisses to you and Ginnie
"Daddy Vic"

P.S. Write soon and tell me all the news, and what you and sister are doing.

Louis V. Connolly[10]

Rosalee wants her father to be remembered for his deep patriotic love for not only America, but also for his sense of duty and service. She also wants him to be known for how much he loved his daughters and how much they treasured him as a father, as a role model, and as a soldier.

---

*"I like to see a man proud of the place in which he lives.
I like to see a man live so that his place
will be proud of him."*

*~ Abraham Lincoln*

---

# PRIVATE
# GERARD L. DESROCHES

*60ᵗʰ Infantry Battalion, 9ᵗʰ Armored Division*
*KIA March 16, 1945*
*Medals: Purple Heart*
*Serial #31462328*
*Plot D Row 2 Grave 31*

Written by Robert Guerin, son of Dorilla Desroches Guerin:

Gerard Lambert Desroches was born on the 22th of February 1908, in Boucherville, Quebec, Canada to parents Arthur Desroches and Marie Elzie Pelletier. According to a picture my mother, Dorilla Desroches Guerin, had, Gerard came from a very large family of six sisters and nine brothers. The married names of the sisters according to an obituary notice my mother had are: Marie Languerand, Lina

(Photo courtesy of Robert Guerin.)

(Photo courtesy of Robert Guerin.)

St Pierre, Cecile Jarry, Jeanne Langeliere, Therese Girouard, and Maria Jarry. Six brothers also named in the obituary notice, which was about 1975, were Arthur, Alphonse, Zenon, Joseph, Vincent, and Edras. The other three brothers, including Gerard, were not mentioned. The Desroches family lived in St. Hyacinthe, Quebec, Canada.

As a young man, Gerald came to St. Albans, Vermont. For twelve years, up to the time of his departure for the Army, he was an employee of St. Albans Grain Company. I really can't be any help about Gerard's personality other than by looking at the many pictures my mother had. Gerard looked to be a very happy and a loving man. And why not? He was married for ten years to my mother, Dorilla. On June 24, 1935, Dorilla Eva Remillard, daughter of Auzilda and Sylva Remillard, and Gerard were united in marriage at Holy Angels Catholic church in St. Albans. (My mother was not particularly fond of the name Dorilla, so Marie was on the marriage record.) They lived in a small apartment in the upstairs of a house near the church. I don't know of anything of their life during this time other than they did not have any children, but they did have a small white dog by the name of Snowball whom they both loved dearly. I remember my mother saying that Snowball died in April of 1945, after Gerard was killed, and that Gerard had come for Snowball.

Gerard left for the service on Good Friday, April 7, 1944. He first went to Fort Devens, Massachusetts, followed by training at Camp Wheeler near Macon, Georgia. My mother was with him for a period of time during Gerard's training. Pvt. Desroches, 31462328, arrived in France in January 1945. He was a rifleman with Company C of the 60th Infantry Battalion of the 9th Armored Division. He was killed in action on March 16, 1945, during a drive east of the Rhine River in Germany when he was struck in the back by enemy small arms fire.

My mother was very hurt by the news of her husband's

**Pvt. Desroches Now Missing, Wife Informed**

Pvt. Gerald L. Desroches has been missing in action in Germany since March 16, his wife, Dorilla, 253 Lake Street, has been advised by the War Department.

He went into the Army a year ago and had been overseas since January. He was serving with the Ninth Army.

Pvt. Desroches was born in St. Hyacinthe, Que., 37 years ago and came to St. Albans as a young man. For 12 years, up to the time of his departure, he was an employe of the St. Albans Grain Company. His parents, Mr. and Mrs. Joseph Desroches, are living at St. Hyacinthe.

**Pvt. Desroches, First Reported Missing, Dead**

Pvt. Gerald L. Desroches, previously reported missing in action March 16 in Europe, actually was killed, according to new word received from the War Department by his wife, Dorilla, of Lake Street.

Pvt. Desroches leaves besides his wife, his parents, Mr. and Mrs. Joseph Desroches of St. Hyacinthe, Que.

Born in St. Hyacinthe 37 years ago, Pvt. Desroches came to St. Albans as a young man. For 12 years he had been an employe of the St. Albans Grain Company, entering the armed forces about a year ago. He had been overseas since January.

death. But like so many others, their faith in God, family, and friends helped her to heal. A memorial mass was held at Holy Angels church where a blessed flag was presented to my mother by the American Legion. I still have this flag.

Many years later, I have returned as an adult to St. Albans. In the town park there is a memorial to the area's war casualties. It states "In memory of those who sacrificed their lives for democracy that they shall not have died in vain." There under World War II is Gerard Desroches' name. Being in the town of my mother's early life and seeing Gerard's name made me very emotional. The memory of Gerard's death is more than just the supreme sacrifice in helping to end a truly evil period of history. It is the memory of family and friends, love and hope. There are similar memories attached to all our war dead. They all had family and friends, love, and hope.[1]

---

*"When we assumed the Soldier,*
*we did not lay aside the Citizen."*

*~ George Washington*

---

# PRIVATE
# JAMES O. DURKEE

*271th Infantry, 69ᵗʰ Division*
*KIA February 19, 1945*
*Medals: Purple Heart*
*Serial #31462366*
*Plot E Row 2 Grave 76*

For Ralph and Beatrice (Goodrich) of Norwich, Vermont, Christmas of 1924 came four days late with the birth of their first child, a son they named James Oliver, who was born on December 29.[1] By 1940, James was the eldest of nine children with five brothers and three sisters. Another brother was born in 1945 and, twenty-five years after giving birth to James, Beatrice gave birth to her last child, a son Kenneth, in 1949.[2] Following grammar school, James earned money by using his talent of carpentry work.[3]

Ralph and Beatrice's two oldest sons, James and Heman, fought in WWII.[4] James entered the Army on April 7, 1944, and served with the 271th Infantry Regiment of the 69ᵗʰ Division. His brother, Heman, served his country from the waters of the Pacific Ocean. The soldier and sailor, so far from home in February 1945, gained a new baby brother on February 3, 1945.[5] One month after greeting her new son Howard, Beatrice received notification that her firstborn

(Photo courtesy of Jacquie Durkee.)

son, James, had been listed as missing in action in Hollerath, Germany.[6] While the Durkee family awaited news about James, the United States Army was attempting to identify unknown deceased soldiers. Among these deceased was Unknown X-473. The following information is supplied in a letter dated March 20, 1945, to the commanding general of the 69th Infantry Division:

1.  Report of burial for Unknown X-473, U.S. Military Cemetery #1, Henri-Chapelle, Belgium, indicates that Lt. King, Graves Registration Officer, 271st Infantry Regiment, has information concerning the identity of this deceased, but that the remains had to be evacuated before the information could be delivered to the collecting point to accompany the remains to the cemetery.

2. Deceased's jacket, underwear, trousers and shoes were marked "D-2366".
3. Place of death of deceased was Hollerath, Germany, and date of death is estimated to be 5 March 1945.
4. Request that any information available concerning the identity of this deceased be forwarded to this headquarters.[7]

Unknown X-473 was identified on June 9, 1945, by fingerprints submitted to the FBI by the Quartermaster General's Office. His name was James Oliver Durkee. Date of death was also changed from March 5, 1945, to February 19, 1945. Beatrice Durkee received notification in July.[8] Private James Durkee never had the opportunity to meet brothers Howard or Kenneth.

Few American families have been untouched by war. The Durkee family of Norwich, Vermont, is not one of those families. Ralph and Beatrice's sons bravely fought in World War Two, Korea, and Vietnam. They are: James and Heman, WWII; Leonard and William, Korea; Kenneth, Vietnam.[9] One has to wonder what Beatrice thought when her firstborn son received his draft notification for World War Two and when her last born son received his draft notification for Vietnam.

---

*"If you are ashamed to stand by your colors, you had better seek another flag."*

*~ Unknown*

---

# PRIVATE
# ALBERT J. GAUTHIER

*36th Infantry Regiment, 3rd Armored Division*
*KIA September 21, 1944*
*Medals: Purple Heart*
*Serial # 31403570*
*Plot B Row 10 Grave 25*

He was born on April 16, 1923, a Monday, in Lacolle, Quebec.[1] A month earlier in March, the German Supreme Court had ruled to prohibit the formation of the Nazi Party.[2] From Lynn and David Gauthier:

> Albert was the oldest of five children born to Elidor and Adelia (Duquette) Gauthier. He came to the US with his parents (his father was born in Canada, his mother in Massachusetts) and three younger siblings--all born in Canada. His youngest sister Lea was born in the US. His parents eventually settled in Essex Junction, VT. Albert's parents eventually saved enough money to buy their own farm and settled in Essex Junction in the early 1940s. At the time of his death they were living in Essex Junction on Kellogg Rd. Albert never married and had no children. His

QMGMR 293
Gauthier, Albert J.
A.S.N. 31 403 570

14 January 1947

Mr. Elidor Gauthier

Essex Junction, Vermont

Dear Mr. Gauthier:

Inclosed herewith is a picture of the United States Military
Cemetery Henri-Chapelle, Belgium, in which your son, the late
Private Albert J. Gauthier, is buried.

It is my sincere hope that you may gain some solace from this
view of the surroundings in which your loved one rests. As you can
see, this is a place of simple dignity, neat and well cared for.
Here, assured of continuous care, now rest the remains of a few of
those heroic dead who fell together in the service of our country.

This cemetery will be maintained as a temporary resting place
until, in accordance with the wishes of the next of kin, all remains are either placed in permanent American cemeteries overseas
or returned to the Homeland for final burial.

FOR THE QUARTERMASTER GENERAL:

Sincerely yours,

1 Incl
  Photograph

ERT

G. A. HORKAN
Brigadier General, QMC
Assistant

mother, Adelia, took his death very hard and chose to have him buried overseas.[3]

He completed grammar school and worked on the family farm.[4]

Albert entered the military three days after Christmas on December 28, 1943.[5] His two younger brothers, Leo and Wilfred, also served in World War Two, Leo with the Army and Wilfred in the Navy. Both survived.[6] Private Gauthier served with the 36th Infantry Regiment of the 3rd Armored Division and was killed in action on September 21, 1944, in Germany.[7]

From his death notice published in *The Suburban List* on October 26, 1944:

Pfc. Albert Gauthier, son of Mr.& Mrs. Elidor Gauthier, of this village, was killed in action in Germany, on September 23, according to the war department. Prior to his enlistment, he was a farmer. Wilfred, a brother, S.2/c, is in the Navy. Leo, another brother, is at home. Besides those named above Albert is survived by two sisters, Lea and Ida.[8]

Private Albert Gauthier's family wants him to be remembered "as a compassionate young man who, as the oldest son, did a lot for his mother and looked after her and the rest of the family. He would help tend the farm, especially when his father was not at home. He felt that as the eldest it was his duty to protect his family and his country."[9]

--------------------------

*"We are citizens of the world.*
*The tragedy of our times is that we do not know this."*

*~ Woodrow Wilson*

--------------------------

# PRIVATE FIRST CLASS
# THEODORE G. HALL

*16th Infantry Regiment, 1st Division*
*KIA March 24, 1945*
*Medals: Purple Heart*
*Serial # 31399924*
*Plot C Row 5 Grave 3*

Theodore "Ted" Graham was born on April 9, 1921, in Pittsfield, Massachusetts, to parents Horace and Hazel (Servis) Hall.[1] He was the oldest of four children with one sister and two brothers.[2] The Hall family moved to Jefferson, Maine, prior to the 1940 census, where Ted completed four years of high school.[3] He moved to Springfield, Vermont, while his parents and siblings remained in Maine. There he met his future wife, Helen Baker, and the two wed on November 7, 1942, in Springfield, Vermont.[4]

Ted Hall entered the military on November 9, 1943, a year after his wedding to Helen, in Portland, Maine.[5] He served with the 16th Infantry Regiment of the 1st Division and was killed in action on March 24, 1945, in Westereiser, Germany.[6] His death notice reads:

## Services For Theodore Hall, Killed in Action

Springfield - Memorial services will be held for Pfc. Theodore Graham Hall, husband of the former Helen E. Baker, daughter of Mr. and Mrs. Milton Baker of North Springfield, at the North Springfield Baptist church on Sunday at 3 p.m. The American Legion will participate in the services at which Rev. E.L. Thornton will officiate. The family has requested that no flowers be sent.

Private Hall entered the service in November, 1943, and went overseas in November, 1944, after training in Camp Butner, N.C., Fort Benning, Ga., and Fort Meade, Md. He was killed by the explosion of a German artillery shell in Germany in April, a few days prior to his 24th birthday on April 9. Burial was in Belgium.

Survivors are the serviceman's wife; his parents, Mr. and Mrs. Horace Hall Jefferson, Me; two brothers, Douglas, who is in the Army, and David; and a sister, June, all of Jefferson.

Pvt. and Mrs. Hall were married here on Nov. 7, 1942. Mrs. Hall, who was graduated from Springfield High School in 1942, received the Purple Heart awarded to her husband posthumously.[7]

Helen's sister, Gertrude Baker, remembers:

He was very thoughtful of others and helpful and rescued someone from drowning on the coast of Maine. He came to Springfield specifically because the shops had so much work to offer. He worked at Bryant Grinder and roomed at Mrs. Moore's at Mansion Hill.

Ted dated Helen's sister Ruth first, but Ruth turned him over to Helen because he was more her type. They lived in a

REMARKS OR ADDITIONAL INSTRUCTIONS *(For additional space use page 4.*)*

*In the booklet "American Cemetries" It is mentioned that cemeteries such as were established after World War I would be established if enough*

AS EXPLAINED IN THE PAMPHLET, "DISPOSITION OF WORLD WAR II ARMED FORCES DEAD," I AM THE NEXT OF KIN AND THE INDIVIDUAL AUTHORIZED TO DIRECT THE DISPOSITION OF THE SAID REMAINS.

**ADDITIONAL REMARKS AND INSTRUCTIONS**
All remarks and information entered here will be considered as part of the Notarial Attestation.

*people wrote and wanted it. I am in favor of the idea.*

*I would like to have my husband stay in Belguim. He liked Belguim very much*

*I read sometime ago that it was talked about having the next of kin go overseas to the cemeteries to see what they are like. I am one who would like this. It would be nice to visit the grave of my husband.*

government trailer in Springfield after marriage and dreamed about having a farm in Maine.[8]

Helen Hall received her husband's personal effects in August of 1945. One item in particular was missing, which prompted her to pen the following letter:

There was one thing in particular I was looking forward to receive. That was his watch. Before he went overseas I bought him a very fine watch. It was shock proof, water proof and ( ) hands and numbers. I have recently heard from a boy that was with my husband when he was hit. He said he saw the watch and it was in perfect condition even after he went down. The watch has sentimental value to it. Do you have any idea as to what became of it? There were a lot of other things he had with him that I didn't get back, but I really wanted the

R.F.D #3 Box 78
Springfield, Vermont
September 14, 1945

476237

dear sir,
I have received the personal things of
my husband P.F.C. Theodore. G. Hall
I got them the middle of August.
There was one thing in particular that
I was looking forward to receive. That
was his watch. Before he went overseas
I bought him a very fine watch. It
was shock proof, water proof and aluminu
hands and numbers. I have recently
heard from a boy that was with my
husband when he was hit. He said
he saw the watch and it was in
perfect condition even after he went
down. The watch has a sentamental
value to it. do you have any idea as
to what become of it? There were a
lot of other things he had with him
that I didn't get back but I really
wanted the watch. The boy said
that Ted always kept the watch
U.S time so the boys knew what
time it was back home.
do you think there's any chance of it
turning up now. The Boy said I should
have gotten it with his things. None
of his smoking things came back but

I'm not so anxious about that as I
am the watch. Please let me know
if there's any hopes of its coming
to me.
many thanks for your kindness

Sincerly
Mrs Helen C Hall
R.F.D #3 Box 78
Springfield, Vermont

watch. The boy said that Ted always kept the watch U.S. time so the boys knew what time it was back home.[9]

"I would like to have my husband stay in Belgium. He liked Belgium very much."[10] Helen Hall's final wish for her husband.

---

*"Remember, Officers and Soldiers, that you are free men fighting for the blessings of liberty."*

*~ George Washington, August 1776*

---

# STAFF SERGEANT
# ARTHUR L. JACOBS

*16ᵗʰ Infantry, 1ˢᵗ Division*
*KIA March 1, 1945*
*Medals: Bronze Star, Purple Heart*
*Serial # 31461870*
*Plot C Row 15 Grave 1*

Arthur Lloyd Jacobs was born on December 9, 1914, to parents Jeremiah and Mary Jane (Brown) of Holland, Vermont.[1] Arthur had two older brothers named Burton and Hughbert along with two older sisters named Mary and Gertrude. The Jacobs family moved to Providence, Rhode Island, in search of employment after Arthur's birth and there the family welcomed the youngest son, Stewart, in 1919.[2] A year later in 1920, they welcomed the last child, a daughter named Caroline. Jeremiah and Mary continued to reside in Rhode Island with their seven children for the next several years until their search for work led them to Hartford, Connecticut.[3]

Arthur completed grammar school before entering the work force.[4] He eventually returned to Vermont's Northeast Kingdom in the early 1930s and there he met his future wife, Beatrice Todd, from a neighboring town just over the Canadian border.[5] The two

SSGT Jacobs, standing second from left, with his siblings.
(Photo courtesy of the Jacobs family.)

soon wed on September 1, 1935, in Derby Line, Vermont.[6] They welcomed their first child, a son, on April 14, 1936, and named him Malcolm Arthur.[7] Their next child, a son they named Sanford, was born on March 9, 1937, in Holland, Vermont. Newborn Sanford died a month later on April 27, 1937.[8] Eleven months after Sanford's birth, a third son arrived on February 16, 1938. Arthur and Beatrice named him Edwin.[9] According to the 1940 census, Arthur and Beatrice resided in Derby, Vermont, with their two boys.[10] The parents welcomed their fourth son, Melvin, on June 27, 1942. At the time of Melvin's birth, "Art", as he was called, was employed as a machinist at the local tap and die factory.[11] Malcolm, Edwin, and Melvin became brothers once again on August 22, 1943. Their parents named her Lorraine. Art's occupation was then farming as listed on Lorraine's birth record.[12] They also still lived in Derby, Vermont.

Art entered the military on April 5, 1944.[13] His youngest brother, Stewart, had entered three years prior on August 7, 1941, whereas his older brother, Hughbert, had entered on July 2, 1942.[14] His oldest brother, Burton, did not serve. Staff Sergeant Jacobs deployed to Europe with the 16th Infantry Regiment of the 1st Division, leaving his four children and pregnant wife. Beatrice delivered her and Arthur's last child on October 30, 1944. Beatrice named her Shiela Ann. Shiela lived for forty minutes before dying from respiratory failure, as stated on her death certificate.[15] Staff Sergeant Jacobs was killed in action four months later on March 1, 1945, in Germany. His two brothers, Stewart and Hughbert, survived the war. Beatrice and Hughbert married on December 6, 1949, in Newport, Vermont.[16] Difficult times struck Beatrice once again with the death of Edwin, her and Arthur's third son, from diabetes on February 7, 1954.[17]

His death notice states:

### Arthur L. Jacobs Reported Killed On Western Front

The War Department advised Mrs. Beatrice (Todd) Jacobs, Hill Street, Newport, Thursday afternoon that her husband, Staff Sergeant Arthur L. Jacobs, 30, was killed in action in Germany, March 1. A non-commissioned officer with an infantry unit of Gen. Hodges' U.S. First Army, S/SGT. Jacobs had been in almost continuous combat duty since last October 27th. He had been in the Army about a year and landed in England last September, going to France in early October.

Besides his widow, he leaves four children: Malcolm, 8; Edwin, 7; Melvin, 2 and Lorraine, 1. He is also survived by Jerry Jacobs of Holland, his father, three sisters, Caroline, who is employed at the Butterfield factory, Derby Line; Mrs. Mary King, Holland; Gertrude Jacobs, Holland; three brothers, Sgt. Stuart Jacobs in Germany, Sgt. Hubert Jacobs in Italy and Burton, Holland.

S/Sgt. Jacobs was born in Orleans, Dec. 9, 1914. For a time his parents lived in Hartford, Conn., where he attended school. At the time he entered the Army he was employed on one of Earl Hackett's Derby farms.

When his two brothers entered the armed forces, Arthur also determined to do his part for his country and help his brothers. Training at Camp Wheeler, Ga., Jacobs went overseas as a private, but his ability and military qualities soon brought recognition and advancement to a staff sergeant's rating.

Current history has recorded the heroic stand made by the out-numbered U.S. First Army in the battle of the "bulge" and its determined comeback to force the Nazis back across the Rhine and during the first week of March crossing that historic water-barrier to bring the war to the vital center of Nazidom.

Like many of his brave companions, none of his letters spoke of hardships or misfortunes. He entered the service of Uncle Sam more than willingly and was determined to do his full part unflinchingly. His last letter to his wife, dated Feb. 22, which arrived in Newport Monday of this week was one of good cheer and spoke pleasurably of having received, on the days previous to the one on which he wrote, several Christmas packages from home.

For his courage and devotion to duty he had received the Bronze Star medal.

It is also a matter of record that both of his brothers had been wounded and were the recipients of the Order of the Purple Heart for wounds received in combat.[18]

Nephew Arthur Jacobs and niece Florence Joyal state their uncle enjoyed hunting, fishing, and dancing. He also possessed a fun, happy, and great overall personality, yet could be tough when necessary. They also share that there existed much confusion about his death, especially for their grandmother, as the family did not know if Hughbert, Arthur, or Stewart had been killed. Confusion ultimately transpired to deep sadness over the loss of Arthur. Florence, Art, and the rest of the Jacobs family want Staff Sergeant Arthur Jacobs to be remembered for his heroic bravery and dedicated service to America as well as to his fellow man.[19]

Parents Jeremiah and Mary Jane.

(Photo courtesy of the Jacobs family.)

---

*"Spirit, that made those heroes dare*
*To die, and leave their children free,*
*Bid Time and Nature gently spare*
*The shaft we raise to them and thee."*

*~ Ralph Waldo Emerson*

---

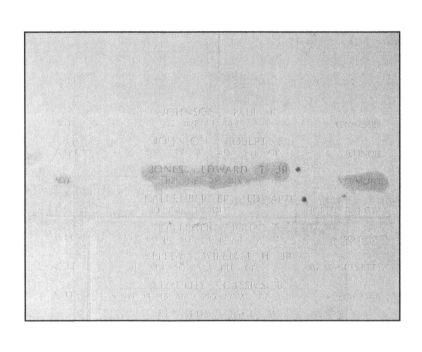

JOHNSON PAUL E.
XXX INF DIV TENNESSEE

JOHNSON ROBERT E.
XX INF XXX LW GT ILLINOIS

JONES EDWARD T JR •
XX INF XX DIV VERMONT

KARLENBERGER EDWARD •
XX INF XX DIV NORTH DAKOTA

KELLHER JOHN E
XX INF XX DIV WISCONSIN

KELLEY WILLIAM H JR
XX INF XX DIV MASSACHUSETTS

KENNEDY CASSIUS B
XX INF XX DIV NEBRASKA

KENNEDY JACK W

# SERGEANT
# EDWARD T. JONES JR

*112th Infantry Regiment, 28th Division Co A*
*KIA November 9, 1944*
*Medals: Bronze Star, Purple Heart*
*Serial # 31020148*
*Our Lady of Mount Carmel Cemetery in*
*Middle Granville, New York*

Edward and Mayme (Whalen) Jones of Pawlet, Vermont, welcomed their second child and first son on October 28, 1917.[1] Named after his father, Edward Thomas Jr. had blue eyes and brown hair.[2] Edward completed three years of high school prior to entering the military on March 14, 1941.[3]

He served with the 112th Infantry Regiment of the 28th Division Co A and was listed as missing in action on November 9, 1944, in the Huertgen Forest in the vicinity of

(Photo courtesy of Delores Luebke.)

Kommerscheidt, Germany.[4]

SGT Jones' parents received the following letter from Major General J.A. Ulio dated April 27, 1945:

> There has been forwarded a letter from overseas, your letter of inquiry concerning your son Sergeant Edward T Jones Jr.
>
> Your distress since he was reported a casualty, and your desire to obtain further information regarding him is most understandable. A report now available in the War Department shows that Sergeant Jones disappeared during the defense and withdrawal of Kommerscheidt, Germany when the enemy counterattacked on 8 November 1944. Your son was appointed Sergeant from Corporal on 8 November 1944, and was serving as assistant squad leader when he was lost.
>
> I wish to assure you that upon receipt of any additional information regarding your son it will be communicated to you immediately. It is regretted that the War Department has no further details as of 18 April 1945.[5]

Major General Edward F. Witsell penned a letter to the family on November 9, 1945. It reads:

> Since your son, Edward T. Jones Jr., 31202148, Infantry, was reported missing in action on 8 November 1944, the War Department has entertained the hope that he survived and that information would be revealed dispelling the uncertainty surrounding his absence. However, as in many cases, the conditions of warfare deny us such information. The record concerning your son shows that he was a member of Company "A", 112th Regiment, 28th Infantry Division, which departed from Kommerscheidt, Germany, south of the Cologne plain, to take and hold Schmidt, Germany. Your son was last seen at Kommerscheidt during an enemy counterattack, but was not present upon reorganization of

the company thereafter.

Full consideration has recently been given to all available information bearing on the absence of your son, including all records, reports and circumstances. They have been carefully reviewed and considered. In view of the fact that twelve months have now expired without the receipt of evidence to support a continued presumption of survival, the War Department must terminate such absence by a presumptive finding of death. Accordingly, an official finding of death has been recorded under the provisions of Public Law 490, 77th Congress, approved March 7, 1942, as amended.

The finding does not establish an actual or probable date of death; however, as required by law, it includes a presumptive date of death for the termination of pay and allowances, settlement of accounts and payment of death gratuities. In the case of your son this date has been set as 9 November 1945, the day following the expiration of twelve months' absence.

I regret the necessity for this message but trust that the ending of a long period of uncertainty may give at least some small measure of consolation. I hope you may find sustaining comfort in the thought that the uncertainty with which war has surrounded the absence of your son has enhanced the honor of his service to his country and of his sacrifices.[6]

On the same day that Major General Witsell wrote the Jones family, Colonel George F. Herbert, Chief of the Casualty Branch, issued the following memorandum concerning the review and determination of status under the Missing Persons Act:

### I. Facts

1. Attached and made part of hereof is a list of 42 military personnel entitled "112th Infantry Regiment Personnel missing in action 8 November 1944, in Germany."

2. These persons were members of various companies in the 112th Infantry Regiment and were reported missing in action 8 November 1944 in Germany by ETO Shipment No. 252 with the exception of Private Gustave J. Seiler, 32891167, who was reported missing in action 8 November in Germany by ETO Shipment No. 254.

3. Combat in the area in which these troops became missing is described as follows by "The World Almanac and Book of Facts for 1945", published by the New York World-Telegram:

"1944—November"

"Nov. 2--***In the Huertgen Forest area United States soldiers took Vossanack and Germeter, south of the Cologne plain.***

"Nov. 3--***United States soldiers advanced two and a half miles and seized Schmidt, but were pushed out the next day by the Germans.***

"Nov. 6--***On the Western Front in the Huertgen area German counterattacks gained half of Vossenack.***

"Nov. 7---***On the Western Front there was heavy fighting in wind-driven rain and icy mud in the Huertgen Forest and the Allies gained in the village of Vossenack—'a heavy German counter-attack broke into the village as far as the church, standing at the crossing of the road from the north to Schmidt with the east-west highway. That village church was the center of bitter fighting. Snipers fired from behind tombstones and the lines were too close for artillery. At times both Americans and Germans were in the same church at once.' Schmidt was still in German possession. German tanks and grenadiers southeast of Stolberg annihilated an American group cut off there and, after heavy battles, captured the locality of Kommerscheidt in the face of fierce enemy resistance.***

"Nov. 8---***In Europe on the Western Front, in the Schmidt area, United States troops were driven from the village of Kommerscheidt, whence they had been launching their repeated attempts to retake Schmidt, 1,000 yards to the southeast. The Americans still clung to Vossenack, although the Germans retained a foothold in the eastern edge of this shattered village.***"[7]

The memorandum continues for Company "A",

a. The following-named men were members of this Company at the time they became missing in action:
> Staff Sergeant John J. Farrell Jr.
> Sergeant Edward T. Jones Jr.
> Private First Class Gordan F. Brader
> Private First Class Carl F. Kime Jr.
> Private First Class Michael Loncar
> Private Frank B. Huggins
> Private Joseph C. Merlock
> Private LeRoy B. Miller Jr.
> Private Isaac D. Privette
> Private Sydney E. Weaver
> Private LeRoy B. Wennevold

b. The following information is revealed by Missing Reports contained in the Casualty Branch files of Staff Sergeant Farrell, PFC Brader, and Privates Huggins, Merlock, Miller, and Privette and the AG 201 files of PFC Kime and Loncar and Privates Weaver and Wennevold:
> The company departed 8 November 1944, from Kommerscheidt to take and hold Schmidt; the above named persons were last known to be at Kommerscheidt. They were "lost during the defense of and withdrawal of Kommerscheidt during enemy counterattack" and were absent upon "reorganization

of Company. No search could be conducted as area in which they were missing was in enemy hands."

c.  The AG 201 file of Sergeant Jones contains a letter dated 19 December 1944 from the Commanding General, European Theater of Operations, to the Adjutant General, subject: Letters of Inquiry, which forwards a letter of inquiry dated 26 November 1944 from soldier's father, First Wrapper Indorsement to which, dated 11 December 1944, from Headquarters, 112th Infantry Regiment, states in part:

"a.  Soldier disappeared during the defense of and withdrawal of Kommerscheidt, Germany during enemy counterattack.

b.  No search could be conducted at the time as area in which soldier was missing was in enemy hands.

c.  At the time of his disappearance soldier was serving as assistant squad leader with Company A, this Regiment"[8]

The report concludes with the recommendation that the presumed date of deaths for all 42 missing soldiers be November 9, 1945.[9]

Attempts to recover the remains of these men did not cease for another five years. Investigator Corporal Hellmuth E. Willner issued several reports of his findings, each dated in 1950. The first one dated October 19 reads:

During a physical search conducted in the Hurtgen Forest, in compliance with Investigation Directive # 205, dated 12 April 1950, the following was found by the undersigned investigator: One right US Army combat boot with portions of a foot in it, along with one M1 rifle, one prayer book, and one helmet liner. No markings or numbers could be identified on either the combat boot, prayer book, helmet or rifle. The partial remains and other recovered items were turned over to the CIL morgue, 7887 Graves Registration Detachment for processing. The subject remains were assigned SR 630. The recovery was made in the "Wilde Sau", Hurtgen Forest, from a foxhole covered in dirt. The immediate surrounding area was thoroughly searched for additional remains, however, with negative results. It is reported that the area in question was heavily mined and that during the fighting changed hands approximately thirty-six times. The possibility exists that the foot is a part of a remains blown up by a mine and of which the rest may or may not have been recovered or that the remaining parts could have been dissected and scattered by carnivorous animals.[10]

His subsequent report dated November 20, 1950, reads:

Narrative of Investigation
I. Authority:
In compliance with instructions contained in Investigation Directive #205, dated 12 April 1950, an investigation was conducted in the Hurtgen Forest and surrounding area, in an effort to recover the remains of unresolved casualties whose last known whereabouts are reported in said area.

II. Facts & Circumstances:
Records, this headquarters, disclose are approximately two hundred (200) unresolved casualties as having been lost in the area involved and indicate a total of one hundred fifty five (155) unknown deceased (Unidentifiables) were recovered from the appropriate area, thus leaving, theoretically, the remains of forty-five (45) of the aforementioned two hundred (200) unresolved casualities still to be recovered. Virtually every town and village in the

subject area and their surrounding forest districts have been repeatedly searched in connection with the recovery of US deceased; however, in the greater majority of cases, this action proved negative.

III. Findings:

On 20 October 1950, the undersigned investigator and three assistant workers commenced a six week physical search of the area in question. Information was obtained from burgermeisters, forest guards, demining team personnel and local inhabitants as to where the heaviest fighting took place and where American and enemy positions were located. Subsequently, a methodical step by step examination of the terrain was made. Foxholes, trenches, permanent fortified land constructions, field obstacles, and ditches were examined and anything bearing the appearance of an isolated grave was opened and thoroughly searched. Farmers were interrogated and through this it was reported that many foxholes, dugouts, trenches, etc. were situated on their farmlands; however, these areas have since been cultivated and rehabilitated to the point that they no longer bear the appearance of a former battle-ground. For this reason the investigation consisted mainly of searching the demined forest districts in the area. Despite the thoroughness of the investigation, only two remains were recovered. It is believed that the effectiveness of the investigation was greatly reduced to the fact that many of the forest districts are still heavily mined, thus precluding immediate investigation.

These mined areas, according to local officials and demining team personnel, will not be completely demined or considered safe for entry for four or possibly five years from this date. Demining activities have, however, been in operation since the end of hostilities and some of the areas are classified as "partially demined." It is reported, by demining teams, that there are areas in which demining activities have not yet been commenced, due to the fact that initial attempts to enter these areas resulted in frequent blow-up and the death of some of their personnel. Personnel of the demining teams added further that there were instances in which the remains of war-time deceased were recovered from the mined areas. However, a thorough review of records, this headquarters, reveals that the remains of US Deceased recovered from the aforementioned mined areas were generally in an incomplete condition and, in most cases, without sufficient identifying media. It was further learned that the forest area is literally infested with wild bears and carnivorous animals that will devour or dissect and scatter a human remains. A minute perusal of Town Hall records and a routine interrogation were conducted at Gresseneich, Grosshau, Kleinhau, Hurtgen, Mausbach, Raffelsbrand, Germeter, Vossenack, Simonskall, and Zweifallshammer; however, with negative results. Only after all possible efforts had been employed and every available means exhausted was this investigation terminated.

IV. Conclusions:
In view of the foregoing, it is concluded that further investigation in those areas not mined or those already demined would not result in the recovery of any the subject unresolved causalities. It is further concluded that any attempt to conduct a thorough search of the mined areas would be costly, timely, and above all extremely dangerous.

V. Recommendations:
Recommend non-recoverable action be initiated.[11]

Mr. and Mrs. Edward Jones received notification on October 9, 1951, seven years after he went missing, that their son's remains were classified as non-recoverable.[12] Both died not ever knowing what happened to their son. Mary Jones Pecue, SGT Jones' sister, kept a hopeful vigil about her brother's return until her death in 2001.[13] Seven years later in 2008, a German ordnance team working at a construction site in Kommerscheidt found pieces of a military boot. SGT Jones finally returned home in 2010:

### 66 years later, a bittersweet homecoming

Recently found remains of World War II soldier who died in Germany being buried in Granville cemetery

Mary Pecue waited most of her life for her brother, Edward Jones, to come home from World War II. Told by the military in 1944 that Jones was missing in action, Pecue had for decades clung to the hope that the Army sergeant had started a family abroad or developed amnesia from a combat injury. She observed a sort of decades-long vigil in her West Pawlet, Vt., home, where she kept a picture of the decorated soldier in her living room so she could see it each day. Pecue reminisced about her brother to friends and family, and dreamed of seeing him walk through her door again, neighbor Delores Luebke recalled.

"She never, never gave up hope," Luebke said. "It really dominated her life."

But Pecue died in 2001 at age 87. Nine years later, her brother has finally arrived.

In what's being described by family as a bittersweet homecoming, uniformed military officials delivered Jones' remains in a flag-draped casket Thursday to the Robert King Funeral Home in the bordering New York community of Granville, where Jones attended high school.

The soldier from the Greatest Generation will be buried

with full military honors at 10 a.m. Saturday in Our Lady Mount Carmel Cemetery in Granville.

Jones, it turns out, died at the age of 27 on Nov. 6, 1944, when a German tank fired "point-blank" at him and five other soldiers with the Army's 112th Infantry Regiment in the town of Kommerscheidt, the Department of Defense POW/Missing Personnel Office announced Thursday.

The Washington County serviceman had fought in the early stages of the nearly five-month Battle of the Hurtgen Forest near the border of Belgium. The fight in the 50-square-mile fir-treed forest raged from October 1944 to February 1945, and is known as the longest continually fought battle in Army history. Marked by cold, wet and sometimes snowy weather, it ended with 24,000 Americans killed, missing, captured or wounded, and another 9,000 who died from trench foot, respiratory diseases and combat fatigue.

Jones was killed about a month before the Battle of the Bulge while moving east in an attempt to capture the towns of Vossenack and Schmidt, the military says.

Nearly 64 years later, on Sept. 25, 2008, a German explosive ordnance disposal team working at a construction site in Kommerscheidt found fragments of an old U.S. military boot. Members of the German War Graves Commission worked at the site and recovered remains, identification tags and equipment belonging to two U.S. soldiers... Jones' entire skeletal remains, Social Security card, helmet, rifle, watch, compass, boots, uniform and Catholic symbols were found in a giant bomb crater, his nephew and Pecue's son, Charles Pecue of Hudson Falls, said. He had never met his uncle, but said Friday that Jones liked to hunt and fish and was known as a hard worker.

"All I ever got from my mother was that he was missing in action and they received his Purple Heart (medal)," Charles

Pecue, 63, said in a short interview Friday. "It's kind of too bad that my mother -- his sister -- passed away already."

Jones had a "sunny personality," said Luebke, his neighbor.

John Norton, an 86-year-old Navy World War II veteran from Granville, recalled Jones as a quiet kid from a warm family whose parents worked in the slate quarries. "We grew up in the Great Depression," Norton said. "Everyone was poor."

Thirty-one men from the Granville school district died in World War II, "which is a lot for a small town like this, Norton said. He said he was thrilled to hear that Jones' remains had been found, and would attend the service.

More than 400,000 Americans died in World War II, including 74,000 who were unable to be recovered, identified or buried and remain unaccounted for, according to the Department of Defense. The U.S. Army Central Identification Laboratory, opened in 1976 in Hawaii, is tasked with recovering and identifying all U.S. service members killed in past wars.

Historians recall the Battle of the Hurtgen Forest as a costly, and ultimately unproductive, struggle that is over-shadowed by the U.S. victory in the Battle of the Bulge. American forces enjoyed a numerical advantage over the enemy, but were hampered by the weather, towering 75- to 100-foot trees and limited use of tanks and air power. In the end, the forest captured was of little strategic or tacti-cal value to future operations, reports say.

But Charles Pecue, a longtime Army veteran, won't be second-guessing military tactics this weekend. The car sales consultant is bringing his wife, son, two daughters and other family members to witness as his fallen un-cle is laid to rest in American soil more than six decades after he was killed in Germany. The Army private who was found alongside Jones will be buried in Cleveland Saturday, too.

"This is very important to me and everyone else," Charles Pecue said. "Another soldier is coming home, and the family is back together."[14]

An article from the Associated Press:

### Remains of WWII soldier from Vt. to be buried

MONTPELIER, Vt.—A World War II soldier from Vermont who was killed in Germany will be laid to rest Saturday, 66 years after his parents learned he was missing in action.

U.S. Army Sgt. Edward T. Jones, of Pawlet, Vt., was part of an infantry regiment that lost six members when a German tank fired on them in November 1944, as U.S. and German troops fought in the Hurtgen Forest along the Germany-Belgium border.

In 2008, an explosive ordnance disposal team working in Kommerscheidt, Germany, found fragments of a boot and notified a war graves commission, prompting the recovery of two soldiers' remains, as well as identification tags.

Jones' relatives learned of the remains in May, when the nephew of the other fallen soldier called.

"It's been a big notch in the family that's been missing for years and now he's back," Jones' great nephew, Charles Edward Pecue IV, 28, of Brighton, Mass., who goes by the name Eddie after the fallen soldier, said Friday.

The news "was exciting and a little strange," said Jones' nephew, Charles Pecue, 63, of Hudson Falls, N.Y., who is also the younger Pecue's father. "You know you're set back a little bit."

Jones, who was 27 when he died, grew up in West Pawlet and liked to hunt and fish, Pecue said. He worked in the slate quarries and went into the service in 1941, before being reported missing in action in 1944, he said.

"All my grandmother told me was that my grandmother and grandfather got a letter from the government saying that Edward was missing in action and they received a Purple Heart," Pecue said.

Jones will be buried with full military honors at Our Lady of Mount Carmel Cemetery in Granville, N.Y., near West Pawlet.[15]

The remains of Staff Sergeant John J. Farrell Jr. of Arlington, Massachusetts, were also found with Sergeant Jones.

### Remains of missing WWII soldier return home for burial
### Arlington native killed 66 years ago in German battle

NORWOOD — For more than six decades, Rosemary Farrell visited a cemetery plot near her childhood home in Arlington with a granite marker but no grave. It was for her older brother, whose fate was known only as the US Army presumed it: death on a German battlefield in 1944.

Yesterday, a military honor guard delivered John J. Farrell Jr.'s remains to his family, 66 years after he went missing in action during the Battle of Hurtgen Forest.

For his loved ones, Farrell's return is an unimagined blessing, a release from years of lingering regret, and a proper chance to say goodbye.

"He's home," said Rosemary Farrell, an 84-year-old who fondly recalls riding on the back of her brother's bike as a young girl. "Home at last."

Tomorrow, Farrell, who was born in 1922, will be laid to rest with full military honors in a family plot in Norwood. An Army blanket will line the casket, and a military uniform will cover his remains.

His return marks another hard-won victory in the painstaking, improbable campaign to recover the far-flung remains of fallen American soldiers in foreign wars.

"I think it's beautiful, in a way," said Barbara Wilson, 85, another sister.

Farrell's remains were discovered in September 2008, when a German explosives team swept a proposed construction site in the village of Kommerscheidt for ordnance left over from one of World War II's longest battles.

After discovering an American combat boot, they excavated the property and found the bones of Farrell, who was a staff sergeant, and another American soldier.

A US team working nearby completed the recovery and transported Farrell's remains to the Joint POW/MIA Accounting Command headquarters in Hawaii to confirm their identity.

The process took months. The Farrell family, meanwhile, learned that Farrell had been honored as a missing soldier at Henri-Chapelle American Cemetery and Memorial, near the Belgian-German border. They contacted military officials and were told that Farrell's body might have been recovered.

Rosemary Farrell and Wilson both submitted DNA samples for confirmation. In September, the call they hoped for finally came.

"It's a miracle," said Rosemary Farrell. "Just imagine, after all these years. It's such a joy, to finally know.''

The family expressed some frustration with the Army over the delay in notifying them, but said they understand the need to be absolutely certain.

Stunningly, Farrell's remains were relatively intact. Excavators found his dog tag and a Waterman fountain pen, which the family imagines he might have used to write letters home. They also found his boots, wallet, and canteen, as well as rifles, grenades, and ammunition.

The Army told Farrell's family that he and several members of his platoon were killed by German tank fire after being surrounded.

Army officials presented the information in person earlier this month at Wilson's Norwood home, a gesture that touched the family.

When Farrell went missing, few details were known. At the time, military officials told the family that he had probably been killed in the Battle of the Bulge and that the chances of finding his remains were slim. They did mention the two central towns in the Battle of Hurtgen Forest, Schmidt and Kommerscheidt.

"I'll never forget those two names," Rosemary Farrell said.

Farrell and Wilson said that the family was devastated by the loss and that their father never entirely recovered.

"Mom lost her husband that day, too," Wilson recalled.

The sisters remember vividly the day the mailman returned letters and packages that were meant for Farrell. Among them was a care package their mother had sent, with rosary beads and socks.

"Isn't that just like a mother?" Wilson said with a wistful smile.

John Farrell Jr. grew up in Arlington, graduating from Arlington High School in 1940. He went on to Boston College, where he studied Latin and Greek.

In 1943, his junior year, he and a group of friends decided to enlist. The following summer, he entered the European Theater. He earned the Purple Heart and the Bronze Star for gallantry in action.

The 1944 Boston College yearbook describes him as a "prankster at heart."

"Life of the party," Wilson said.

"But a good boy," Farrell added.

The sisters said they feel profound relief that his remains at last can be laid to rest in the country he gave his life for.

"There was always something missing," Farrell said. "But we've found him."[16]

---

*"Goodbyes are not forever.*
*Goodbyes are not the end.*
*They simply mean I'll miss you*
*Until we meet again!"*

*~ Author Unknown*

---

# PRIVATE ADELARD JOYAL

*46th Infantry Battalion,*
*5th Armored Division*
*KIA August 21, 1944*
*Medals: Purple Heart,*
     *Bronze Star*

*Serial # 31115319*
*Plot F Row 11 Grave 35*

# STAFF SERGEANT GEORGE E. JOYAL

*18th Infantry Regiment,*
*1st Division*
*KIA January 15, 1945*
*Medals: Purple Heart,*
     *Silver Star,*
     *Bronze Star*

*Serial #31257778*
*Plot F Row 11 Grave 36*

Charles and Orea (Paulus) Joyal of Saint David, Canada, had eight children. Their first five children were born in Canada, including brothers Adelard and George. Adelard, the couple's third-oldest son, was born on January 16, 1918. George Emile, their fourth son and fifth child, was born on July 13, 1920.[1] The Joyal family immigrated to America in 1924, settling first in Rhode Island. The family resided in Burlington, Vermont, by 1930.[2]

Nicknamed "Jim", Adelard was known for his great sense of humor.[3] He completed grammar school and found employment in various semiskilled occupations. Jim entered the military in Vermont

Adelard Joyal

(Photo courtesy of the Joyal family.)

George E. Joyal

(Photo courtesy of the Joyal family.)

on June 25, 1942, as a single man with no dependents.[4]

Whereas Jim possessed a memorable sense of humor, his brother George's personality was more reserved. He attended St. Anthony's grammar school and graduated from Burlington High School in 1938.[5] Three years after graduating from high school, George married Constance "Connie" Mable Gorman on August 30, 1941, in Burlington, Vermont.[6] Mr. and Mrs. George Joyal moved to Massachusetts for employment purposes.[7] Six months after Jim entered the military, George entered on December 22, 1942, in Massachusetts.[8]

Jim served with the 46th Infantry Battalion, 5th Armored Division and died of wounds he received in action on August 21, 1944, in Breval, France. He was interred at the temporary American military cemetery in St. Corneille, France.[9] At the time of his death, Private Joyal possessed sixty-two family photos.[10]

Two weeks after his brother's death, George wrote the following home to family from Ft. Meade:

Dear Lu, Emma, and Kids:

Just a few lines to let you know that everything is O.K. by me.

I've been here two days now and don't think I'd like to stay here. I may not be here long. They stay from 10 days to two weeks. We've been issued new equipment.

I hope Connie is O.K. She was feeling pretty blue when I left her at the station. I got here in plenty of time.

You can write to this address. I'll get it alright.

How are the boys getting along?

Answer soon,

George"

Connie

(Photo courtesy of the Joyal family.)

George E. Joyal

(Photo courtesy of the Joyal family.)

Adelard Joyal

(Photo courtesy of the Joyal family.)

Staff Sergeant Joyal served with the 18<sup>th</sup> Infantry Regiment, 1<sup>st</sup> Division and was killed in action on January 15, 1945, in Belgium. He died one day prior to what would have been his brother's 27<sup>th</sup> birthday. His widow, Connie, remarried and moved to New York.[12] Charles and Orea decided to have their two sons permanently interred next to one another at Henri-Chapelle.

Nephew George Joyal reflects about his two uncles, "George and Adelard should be remembered as two patriots who answered the call and gave their lives for America, as did thousands of other sons and husbands."[13]

---

*Executive Mansion, Washington, November 21, 1864.*
*Mrs. Bixby, Boston, Massachusetts:*

*Dear Madam: I have been shown in the files of the War Department a statement of the Adjutant-General of Massachusetts that you are the mother of five sons who have died gloriously on the field of battle. I feel how weak and fruitless must be any words of mine which should attempt to beguile you from the grief of a loss so overwhelming. But I cannot refrain from tendering to you the consolation that may be found in the thanks of the Republic they died to save. I pray that our Heavenly Father may assuage the anguish of your bereavement, and leave you only the cherished memory of the loved and lost, and the solemn pride that must be yours to have laid so costly a sacrifice upon the altar of freedom.*
*Yours very sincerely and respectfully,*

*Abraham Lincoln.*

---

# PRIVATE FIRST CLASS
# HOWARD D. LAPAN

*60th Infantry Regiment, 9th Infantry Division*
*DOW March 1, 1945*
*Medals: Purple Heart*
*Serial # 31470028*
*Plot F Row 1 Grave 24*

Howard Douglas was born on May 5, 1923, to Ernest and Eliza (Patch) Lapan of Johnson, Vermont.[1] He was the couple's third child and son and would become an older brother to sister Eliza.[2] He worked on a farm and completed one year of high school.[3] His cousin was Shirley Patch, the future wife of PFC Royal Rufus, who also rests at Henri-Chapelle.[4] His father, Ernest, died on January 9, 1936.[5]

Howard entered the military on June 12, 1944, and served with the 60th Infantry Regiment, 9th Infantry

(Photo courtesy of Jerry Schuebel.)

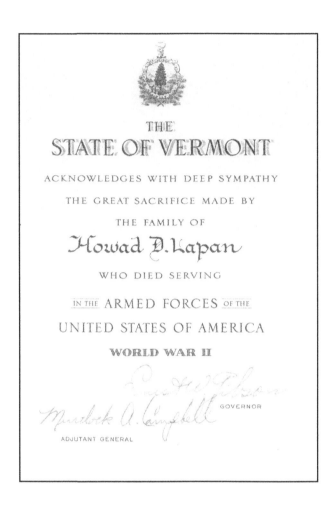

THE

# STATE OF VERMONT

ACKNOWLEDGES WITH DEEP SYMPATHY

THE GREAT SACRIFICE MADE BY

THE FAMILY OF

*Howad D. Lapan*

WHO DIED SERVING

IN THE ARMED FORCES OF THE

UNITED STATES OF AMERICA

**WORLD WAR II**

GOVERNOR

ADJUTANT GENERAL

Division.[6] He died on March 1, 1945, at a field hospital in Germany from wounds received in action.[7] PFC Lapan's death notice reads:

### Pfc. Howard LaPan died of wounds received February 28 in Germany

Private LaPan is the son of Mrs. Howard C. Stevens of Elmore. He was 21 years old, was born in Johnson, and later lived in Stowe and Elmore.

He received his training at Camp Wheeler, Ga., and arrived in Europe in October, 1944, where he had been in active duty in Holland, Belgium, and Germany. He has an older brother, Sergt. William C. LaPan with the 43 Division, 172nd Infantry somewhere in the Philippians. He was a survivor of the Calvin Coolidge and has served for 32 months in the South Pacific area.[8]

---

*"All those soldiers belong to somebody.*
*They got moms, they got wives, they got kids. . . .*
*They got somebody who loves them."*

*~ Liz Allen, Vietnam nurse*

---

# CORPORAL
# MAURICE G. METIVIER

*7th Field Artillery Battalion, 1st Infantry Division*
*KIA March 6, 1945*
*Medals: Purple Heart*
*Serial # 11000215*
*Plot A Row 9 Grave 13*

Maurice George was born on June 17, 1908, to George and Dorothy (Dague) of Jericho, Vermont.[1] He had one older sister, Madeline, and four younger siblings.[2] Maurice completed grammar school and two years of high school prior to entering the military on October 29, 1940.[3]

Jose "Dorothy" Nashville said "I do" to Corporal Metivier and together they had two children with only one surviving infancy. Wanda Ann was born on August 18, 1941, in Ludlow, Vermont.[4] Her father, who smoked a pipe, died five months prior to her fourth birthday.

Corporal Metivier served with the 7th Field Artillery Battalion, 1st Division and was killed in action on March 6, 1945, in Weilerswist, Germany.[5] At the time of his death, Dorothy and Wanda resided in Winooski, Vermont.

QMMR 293
Metivier, Maurice G.
A.S.N. 11 000 215

7 January 1947

Mrs. Dorothy G. Metivier
60 Leclair Street
Winooski, Vermont

Dear Mrs. Metivier:

Inclosed herewith is a picture of the United States Military
Cemetery Henri-Chapelle, Belgium, in which your husband, the late
Corporal Maurice G. Metivier, is buried.

It is my sincere hope that you may gain some solace from this
view of the surroundings in which your loved one rests. As you can
see, this is a place of simple dignity, neat and well cared for.
Here, assured of continuous care, now rest the remains of a few of
those heroic dead who fell together in the service of our country.

This cemetery will be maintained as a temporary resting place
until, in accordance with the wishes of the next of kin, all remains are either placed in permanent American cemeteries overseas
or returned to the Homeland for final burial.

FOR THE QUARTERMASTER GENERAL:

Sincerely yours,

1 Incl
   Photograph

GEO. A. HORKAN
Brigadier General, QMC
Assistant

tJh

*C E R T I F I C A T E*

I certify that all Government property except articles prescribed by (3)
current regulations has been removed and turned-in to Unit Supply, and
that this _____ Card-board box _____ (4)
contains only personal belongings listed below (continue on reverse side (5)
if necessary):

1ea Camera. (Falcon)                                              (6)
4 ea. Pipes                        Personal Letters
5 ea. Rolls, Films                 Personal Pictures
2 ea. Rosaries                     6 ea. Souvenir Coins           (7)
1 ea. Tobacco Pouch                1 pr. Dice (Souvenir )
1 ea. Cigarette case
1 ea. Military Missile
1 ea. Cribbage Board reverse side

        Check List
Letter is signed by an officer.   :
All blanks properly accomplished. :          R.J. NELSON
Property is securely packed.      :          (Name)         (Rank)
Containers are marked with full   :          Captain, 7th F.A. Bn.,
particulars concerning owner.     :          Commanding.
                                                  (Title)
        To be filled-in by receiving organization

His death notice states:

## Corp. M. Metivier Of Winooski Killed in Action

Mrs. Maurice Metivier of Weaver Lane was notified yesterday that her husband, Corp. Maurice Metivier was killed in action in Germany, March 6. The telegram received from the war department read as follows: "The secretary of war desires to express his regret that your husband, Corp. Maurice Metivier, was killed in action in Germany, March 6. Confirming letter follows."

Corp. Metivier had been in the service since Oct. 1940, as a member of the seventh field artillery, formerly of Fort Ethan Allen. He received his training at Camp Blanding, Fla., and Indiantown Gap, Penn., from where he left to go overseas in Aug. 1942. Before moving on to Germany, Corp. Metivier was in Africa, where he took part in the African campaign.

He is survived by his widow, the former Dorothy Nashville of Bedford, P. Q., his daughter, Wanda Ann, his parents, Mr. and Mrs. George Metivier; three sisters, Mrs. Madeline Miller, Mrs. Thelma Szydlo of Portsmouth, N.H., and Natalie; one brother, First Class Petty Officer Arnold Metivier, now somewhere in the Pacific.[6]

Niece Gerry Eggleston states, "He was very loved and admired by all of his family."[7]

------------

*"Courage is rightly esteemed the first of human qualities because it is the quality which guarantees all others."*

*~ Winston Churchill*

------------

# PRIVATE FIRST CLASS
# HAROLD K. MITCHELL

*590th Field Artillery Battalion, 106th Infantry Division*
*KIA December 21, 1944*
*Medals: Purple Heart*
*Serial # 31253298*
*Plot B Row 1 Grave 22*

Harold Kenneth Mitchell was born on January 6, 1923, to William and Beatrice (Dragon) Mitchell of Alburg, Vermont.[1] He had an older sister named Audrey and a younger sister named Shirley.[2] Harold "Buddy" completed one year of high school in Alburg and worked at the Alburg Creamery. His interests included baseball and fishing. Harold possessed an easy-going, humorous personality in addition to being a hard worker.[3] He entered the military on January 13, 1943.[4]

(Photo courtesy of Harold Mitchell Jr.)

Alburg, Vermont.
October 27, 1947.

XC-3 871 779
Mitchell, Harold K.

Quartermaster General's Office
War Department
Washington, D.C.

Gentlemen:

I am enclosing the copy of a letter which I had made up for me by Mr. Howard Sessions at the Veteran's Bureau in Burlington, Vermont.

My daughter-in-law received various papers concerning my son, Harold K. Mitchell. She does not seem to want his body returned to this country but she did promise to give me some of the papers so that I could fill them out and have him brought home. I have never received any papers addressed directly to me concerning this matter so therefore I do not even know where his body will be placed if he is not returned to Alburg. I would at least like this information even though it might be impossible for his body to be returned to this country.

Is there any possible way in which I can claim entitlement to the final disposition of my son's body without my daughter-in-law's signature?

I would greatly appreciate any available information. My son was originally buried in the Henri-Chapelle U.S. Military Cemetery in Eastern Belgium.

Sincerely yours,
Mrs. Beatrice B. Mitchell
Alburg, Vermont.
Box 248.

Private First Class Mitchell married Beulah Mumley on September 16, 1944, at St. Amadeus Church in Alburg.[5] He served with the 590th Field Artillery Battalion of the 106th Infantry Division. Beulah Mitchell received notification on January 16, 1945, that her husband had been reported as missing in action on December 17th in Germany.[6] He was later classified as killed in action on December 21, 1944, in Hunningen, Belgium, just three months after his wedding.[7] His son, Harold Kenneth Mitchell Jr. was born eight months later.[8]

Although father and son never had the opportunity to meet, Harold Jr. recounts the following story, "My father lost an eye in an accident at work. He tried to enlist, but because of the loss of an eye, wasn't able to until near the end of the war. He was only able to join the military because of his persistence."[9]

Beulah Mitchell desired her husband remain interred overseas, whereas PFC Mitchell's mother hoped to bring him home.[10] Beulah waived all entitlements and granted consent for her mother-in-law to be granted full authority as to the final interment of PFC Mitchell.[11] He remained in Belgium.

---

*"Americans never quit."*

*~ Douglas MacArthur*

---

# TECHNICIAN FIFTH CLASS RAYMOND H. MUIR

*46th Infantry Battalion, 5th Armored Division Co B*
*KIA December 16, 1944*
*Medals: Bronze Star, Purple Heart*
*Serial #31020065*
*Plot B Row 11 Grave 46*

Sandy and Nellie Margaret (Handly) Muir of Sharon, Vermont, welcomed their first child on June 11, 1917.[1] They named him Raymond Handly. The Muir family eventually expanded to include seven more children.[2] His obituary published in the *White River Herald* reads:

> Mr. and Mrs. Sandy Muir received a telegram from the War Department Sunday morning, Jan. 7th, telling them that their son, Cpl. T-5 Raymond, had been killed in action on Dec. 16th in Germany.
>
> Cpl. Raymond Handly Muir was born in Sharon June 11, 1917, the oldest child of Sandy and Nellie Margaret (Handly) Muir. He graduated from grammar school in 1932.

(Photo courtesy of John A. Anderson.)

Sharon Vt.
July 1st 1946.

Quartermaster
General U. S. Army
Washington 25. D C.
Dear Sirs; -
My son T/5.
Raymond H Muir
a. S. N. 31,620,605
is buried in the
U. S. military cemetery
in Henri Chapelle Belgium
I would rather
have the Government
furnish me with
a head stone to be
put in our family

lot here in Sharon
as to have his body
brought home.
His request was if
he was killed over
there to be buried
over there.
Yours Truly
Mrs Nellie Muir
Sharon Vt.

Raymond spent 15 months in two different CCC camps and then he worked on the Vermont highway until he entered the service on March 11, 1941, going to Camp Wheeler, Ga., and Camp Blanding, Fla.

He went overseas in January, 1942, to Camp Clayton, Canal Zone. He returned to the States in March, 1943. He left Camp Kilmer, N.J., last February for England.

Raymond leaves, besides his parents, three brothers and four sisters -Margaret M., Mrs. James Bullard of this town; Alexander J., at home; Mary A., Mrs. Nelson Parizo of Claremont, N.H.; Janet N. and Marshall W., at home; also his grandfather, James Handly, of Claremont. He was engaged to Miss Gladys E. Chadwick of Perkinsville.

Raymond was a fine young man and full of promise. All he was looking forward to was to get the job over and come home to his little farm in the Day district.[3]

Initially reported as missing in action on November 30, 1944, Technician Fifth Class Muir was later listed as killed in action on December 16, 1944, in Germany.[4] In a letter to the Quartermaster General of the US Army dated July 1, 1946, Nellie Muir writes, "His request was if he was killed over there to be buried over there."[5]

---

*The muffled drum's sad roll has beat*
*The soldier's last tattoo*
*No more on life's parade shall meet*
*That brave and fallen few;*
*On Fame's eternal camping ground*
*Their silent tents are spread;*
*But Glory guards with solemn round*
*The bivouac of the dead.*

*~ Theodore O'Hara, 1847*

---

# PRIVATE
# HARVEY COLTON OLIVER

*41ˢᵗ Infantry Regiment, 2ⁿᵈ Armored Division*
*DOW December 24, 1944*
*Medals: Purple Heart with Oak Leaf Cluster*
*Serial # 31340858*
*Plot G Row 8 Grave 19*

Harvey Colton Oliver was born on July 17, 1925, in South Carolina to Charles and Olive (Colton) Oliver.[1] He was named after his maternal grandfather and was the couple's only child.[2] The Oliver family moved to Manchester, Connecticut,[3] before eventually settling in Olive's hometown of Fairlee, Vermont, by 1940.[4]

Harvey completed four years of high school before entering the military on September 29, 1943.[5] He served with the 41ˢᵗ Infantry Regiment of the 2ⁿᵈ Armored Division and died of wounds received in action on December 24, 1944, at a field hospital in Belgium, at the age of nineteen.[6]

An excerpt from *The Town Under the Cliff: A History of Fairlee, Vermont*:

> The victory was won, it was supposed, and Fairlee along with the rest of the world was allowed to return to doing

Fairlee, Vermont
December 28, 1945.

Personal Effects Department
U.S. Army, Kansas City, Mo.

Dear Sir:

Our son Private Harvey C. Oliver was wounded on Dec. 24th, 1944 and died the same day at Base Hospital No. 50 at Liege, Belgium and was buried on Dec. 25th in the cemetery at Fosse, Belgium. He was a private in Co. F, 41st Armored Infantry 2nd Armored Division.

We have never received his personal effects. He should have had on his person a good Swiss wrist watch, a fountain pen, a bill fold and other things. The families of most casualties we have known about have received the personal effects within two to four months. Our son has now been buried over a year. It would help to assuage

silent heartache of his [...] if we could have those [...] that will mean so much [...] and to me.

[...] when his outfit left England [...] in July 1944 they were ordered [...] behind one duffel bag in [...] Harvey had several personal [...] including two sweaters. [...] would that be at Depot Q 290 - E.T.O?

I will greatly appreciate a prompt reply to this inquiry.

Charles Oliver
Fairlee, Vermont.

re Private Harvey C. Oliver 31 340 858
Co. F. 41st Armored Infantry
2nd Armored Division
A.P.O. 252

its own quiet task in the cycle we call human life. Peace seemed to be really accomplished for almost a quarter of a century. Again, however, the clouds were to gather and the crazed mind of Adolph Hitler was to rise in all its madness. Would it ever stop, this raising sons and daughters to be used as cannon fodder to quell maniacal ideas? Again the blare of trumpets and drawing of lots to see who must be the first to go, unless the voluntary enlistment had taken precedence. Fifty-two men and women, almost ten percent, of the town's young were to offer up their life blood for the ideals they held so dear. Their record is nobly written in the list of citations individually won, although personal modesty will not permit the holders to enlarge upon their deeds, crowned by the supreme sacrifice as made by one of the fellows around town in former days, a well-liked, respected youth with the world ahead of him — Harvey Colton Oliver, killed on the field of battle in Belgium December 24, 1944. May his sacrifice not have been in vain!

His memory has been perpetuated by the forming of the Harvey Colton Oliver Post No. 8504, Veterans of Foreign Wars formed in 1946 with an average of about fifty members and its auxiliary in 1947 of some twenty women members.[7]

Charles and Olive requested their son's full name of Harvey Colton Oliver rather than Harvey C. Oliver be inscribed on his cross at Henri-Chapelle.[8]

Private Oliver's death notice reads:

### Fairlee Man Dies in Action

Fairlee, Jan. 16 Pvt. Harvey C. Oliver, 19, only son of Mr. and Mrs. Charles Oliver of this town, was killed in action in Belgium December 24, according to a telegram received tonight by his parents from the War department.

Pvt. Oliver was a member of the class of 1943 at Brandon

EXTRACT COPY

Fairlee, Vermont
February 23, 1945

The Adjutant General
War Department
Washington 25, D. C.

Dear Sir:

I have today received two scrolls from your office.

\*\*\*\*\*\*\*\*\*\*\*\*\*\*\*                                    \*\*\*\*\*\*\*\*\*\*\*\*\*\*

I presume we will receive in due time the record
of his service, battle ribbons and awards to which he
was entitled as well as his personal effects: wrist
watch, fountain pen, private papers, etc.

Very truly yours,

Charles Oliver

High school where his father was formerly a teacher. He was captain of the Brandon High school ski team.

He entered the Army in October, 1943, and received his basic training in the infantry at Fort McCleland, Ala. He was sent overseas in April, 1944.

Pvt. Oliver was with the Second Armored division in September in the liberation of Belgium and was wounded October 6 when the Second Armored made the first penetration of the Siegfried Line.

He was killed on the first day of a four day battle in which his division was praised by Field Marshal Montgomery for stopping the German counter-offensive. This is the famous "hell on wheels division," of which Maj. Gen. Ernest R. Harmon of Newbury is commanding general.[9]

---

*"Men who have offered their lives for their country know that patriotism is not the fear of something; it is the love of something."*

*~ Adlai Stevenson*

---

# PRIVATE
# MAURICE P. PLOOF

*551st Parachute Infantry Regiment*
*KIA January 7, 1945*
*Medals: Purple Heart*
*Serial # 31200681*
*Plot G Row 11 Grave 59*

Treffle and Zepherine (Dubois) of Canada had their third child on April 26, 1924. They named him Maurice Peter.[1] The family of five immigrated to America in 1925, settling in Sheldon, Vermont.[2] Treffle and Zepherine had three more sons and two daughters after Maurice and the Ploof family resided in St. Albans, Vermont, by 1940.[3]

His death notice reads:

### Maurice P. Ploof of St. Albans Reported Killed

St. Albans, January 26- Mr. and Mrs. Treffle Ploof, 51 Hoyt St., received a telegram from the war department yesterday that their son, Private Maurice Peter Ploof, aged 21 years, was killed in action in Belgium on January 7.

Private Ploof, prior to his enlistment in the army on

QMQMR 293
Ploof, Maurice P.
A.S.N. 31 200 681

22 January 1947

Mr. Treffle Ploof
51 Hoyt Street
Saint Albans, Vermont

Dear Mr. Ploof:

Inclosed herewith is a picture of the United States Military
Cemetery Henri-Chapelle, Belgium, in which your son, the late
Private Maurice P. Ploof, is buried.

It is my sincere hope that you may gain some solace from this
view of the surroundings in which your loved one rests. As you can
see, this is a place of simple dignity, neat and well cared for.
Here, assured of continuous care, now rest the remains of a few of
those heroic dead who fell together in the service of our country.

This cemetery will be maintained as a temporary resting place
until, in accordance with the wishes of the next of kin, all remains are either placed in permanent American cemeteries overseas
or returned to the Homeland for final burial.

FOR THE QUARTERMASTER GENERAL:

Sincerely yours,

1 Incl
    Photograph

G. A. HORKAN
Brigadier General, QMC
Assistant

December 9, 1942, was employed as a member of a section crew of the Central Vermont Railway, Inc. He received training as a paratrooper at camps in Alabama, Georgia and North Carolina and had been overseas since April, 1944. Besides in Belgium he saw service in North Africa, Sicily, and France.

Besides his parents he leaves three brothers, Harvey Ploof of Hartford, Conn., Norman and Raymond Ploof of St. Albans; four sisters, Mrs. Yvonne Menard and Mrs. Irene Tahner of Hartford, Conn., and Anita and Rita Ploof of St. Albans.[4]

---

*"The cement of this union is the heart-blood of every American."*

*~ Thomas Jefferson*

---

# CAPTAIN
# RICHARD B. PRENTISS

*668ᵗʰ Bomb Squadron 416ᵗʰ Bomb Group L*
*KIA December 25, 1944*
*Medals: Air Medal with 9 Oak Leaf Clusters*
*Serial # O-789200*
*Plot G Row 14 Grave 15*

A s told by researcher, Patti Johnson:

Richard Burr Prentiss was born 2 February 1916, in Burlington, Chittenden County, Vermont, the son of Dr. Orlow Frederick Prentiss and Marjorie B. (nee Elms) Prentiss. He had an older brother, Robert, and a younger sister, Barbara.

He graduated from High School in Burlington, and attended Green Mountain State College in Poultney, Vermont. He then attended Syracuse University in Syracuse, New York, and enlisted in the U.S. Army Air Corps, as an aviation cadet, on 4 September 1941. He graduated from Syracuse University, in June of 1942.

He was sent for training and became a pilot of A20 Havoc Light Bomber aircraft. He was assigned to the 9th Air Force, 416ᵗʰ Bomb Group, 668ᵗʰ Bomb Squadron.[1]

Captain Prentiss was engaged to be married, according to an entry dated December 14, 1944, in the *Operational History of the 668th Bomb Squadron, 416th Bomb Group:*

> At last it has happened: word was verified today of an occasion we never thought would occur. American girls lost a feather from their caps, when it was learned that a "limey" gal snared Capt. "Rick" Prentiss. A London girl finally roped that dark, suave, pilot. His present plans are to complete his tour over here, and then return to the States with his bride. With him will go our best wishes for a happy future. And so, one more confirmed bachelor hits the dust.[2]

Captain Prentiss was killed in action on Christmas Day 1944, while on a bombing mission to the Ahutte Railhead in Losheim, Germany. From Missing Air Crew Report 11668: "He was flying an A20J-15 with a crew of 4 when it was hit by flak between the IP and the target. The bomber was part of the 416th Bomb Group-L, 668th Bomb Squadron, IX Bomb Div (M) [9th Air Force]. The left wing came off and the bomber spun end over end to the ground. One parachute was seen at 6-7000 feet."[3] Those killed with Captain Prentiss were:

Bomb/Nav: 1Lt. Francis H. Bursiel
~O-749718~Whitman, Essex County, MA

Armorer-Gunner: SSgt. Daniel M. Brown
~35514148~Lakewood, Cuyahoga County, OH

Armorer-Gunner: Sgt. Alvin O. Wylie
~13170122~New Kensington, Westmoreland County, PA[4]

As written in *Attack Bombers, We Need You! A History of the 416th Bomb Group* by Ralph Conte (Pages 181 – 182)

Mission #176 - 25 December - MERRY CHRISTMAS - AM - Munstereifel, Germany. A real sad day for such a joyous celebration. At 0900, the formation took off to bomb an important communication center. As the planes neared Malmedy and Munstereifel, heavy flak greeted them. Colonel Willetts and Lt. Royalty, BN led Box I. Other flights led by Captain Miracle, Lt. Burg, BN - Captain Prentiss, Lt. Burseil, BN, - and Lts. Pair and Corum, BN. On the straight and narrow bomb run, direct hits downed Captain Miracle's plane, he on his 65th mission. Lt. Kehoe of the 669th squadron took another hit, causing his plane to catch fire and go down. One chute was seen to open. In all, the main target was not rendered useless, since flak bursts obscured visibility. Bombardiers selected targets nearby, bridges, and roads, with effect. One plane piloted by Lt. Mooney lost his flight in the clouds, so he tacked on to another flight going in to bomb. Of the seven planes in that flight, only three were still together. Mooney's ship caught 74 flak holes in it.

Lt. Greene of the 669th, on his 65th mission, was hit, but he did manage to get back. Mooney landed with a flat tire, but came out okay. Bombing scored one superior. Two did not bomb the primary and one - no attack.[5]

The story of Captain Prentiss' fate continues in the *Operational History 668th Bomb Squadron (416th Bomb Group (L)) WWII* by Wayne Williams, et.al.

(Photo courtesy of Patti Johnson.)

December 25, 1944

Merry Christmas; in peacetime those words would carry a wonderful feeling. Here, it marked the end of the trail for some of our best boys. Men, who came all the way with us, were lost today, one of the blackest days in the squadron's history. They gave their lives on the very day that signified "peace on earth." Their sacrifices must never be forgotten, and never have to occur in the future generations to come.

Those who won't answer the roll tonite are: Captain Richard B. Prentiss, Captain Richard V. Miracle, 1st Lt. Robert R. Svenson, 1st Lt. Jack J. Burg, 1st Lt. Francis H. Bursiel, S/Sgt. D. M. Brown, S/Sgt. P.G. Fild, Sgt. A.O. Wylie, S/Sgt. John H. Simmons, and S/Sgt. A.F. Galloway. The status of these men is unknown; they may be dead or alive. In many cases, witnesses doubt their chances of being alive. Time will tell, whom fate smiled on.

Very early on this Xmas morning, the formation took off to secure peace and happiness for the future world. Thirty-five aircraft were sent out, six of them containing crews from this squadron. The B/N Team of Miracle & Burg, with Gunners Simmons and Galloway led the second flight of the second box. Flying with them were Lt's Chalmers, Prucha, Montrose, Jacobsen, and Lackner?[sic].

The trip over was mild until nearing the target. Again it was a communications center target, this time at Munstereifel, Germany. Heavy accurate flak came up, and took its toll. Just before the point of releasing bombs, a burst caught Capt. Miracle directly in the bomb-bay. The plane was seen to explode in mid-air, and that was all there was to it.

Thus ended the career of four of the best men to have ever entered the squadron. Capt. Miracle was a West Point graduate, with a very promising future in the air. He had over 55 missions. Fate was against Lt. Burg, as he almost was lost on Capt. Meagher's last flight. S/Sgt. Simmons, young and curly haired, had twenty missions to his credit. S/Sgt. Galloway was on the sure par with Simmons. This was one of the smoothest B/N Teams in operation. Several pilots on the mission claim to have seen one chute come from the plane. A dim ray of hope still shines for one of these men.

Another plane and crew were lost of another squadron. The rest of the formation returned intact to the base, badly riddled. Enemy planes were seen, but didn't attack due to our perfect fighter cover. This mission was of 3:30 duration. Needless to say, everyone felt pretty bad when learning of the news. Xmas had ceased to exist for many. The results were good, with one "superior," two P.N.P., and one "no attack."

Refueling, re-loading and repairing was the order prior to the next mission's takeoff. Ground crews working feverishly had the planes ready in a little over an hour's passing. At just a little past 1400 hours, the next mission was already taking off. This was Group Mission # 177, and was to strike us another hard blow. We had nine crews take part from this squadron, two of them leading both boxes. Captain "Rick" Prentiss, with Lt. Bursiel and Gunners Brown and Wylie, led the first box in an A-20J. Right behind them, leading the second box was Major Price, with Lt. Hand and Gunners Fild at the .50 cals. This was Fild's 51st mission, and upon return he would return to the States. These are the twists of fate that cut deep.

The target was the defended village of Hillsheim, Germany. Again, all of this bombing was done to put a crimp in Von Runstedt's drive. The flight over was quiet, till the target area was reached. Then all hell broke loose, the effects—devastation. "Rick" Prentiss rocked his plane all over the sky in evasive action, but to no avail. The flak was heavy and intense, and clawed at the planes in the sky. Bursts of flak surrounded Prentiss's plane, and also caught his wingman and deputy. Both were seen going down, with no

(Photo courtesy of Patti Johnson.)

chutes blossoming. They crashed, and no one escaped to the knowledge of the eyewitnesses. "Rick" Prentiss was to be married in three months. He had over 45 missions to his credit, holder of the Air Medal and DFC. "Frank" Bursiel was one of those dependable bombardiers and an excellent officer. S/Sgt Brown was Chief Gunner of the squadron, and was doing a great job. It was Wylie's second mission, and he was eager always. "Swede" Svenson was always sweating them out to get back to Ohio and the Mrs. Fild was happy in the fact that it was his last, and he too would be able to go home to Ohio. Christmas will be remembered by many this year.

The rest of the formation made it back to the base after dropping their loads. They were very battered and broken up, and both Major Price and Lt. "Buck" Buchanan couldn't bring their planes back to the area. They had to be towed back. The flight lasted 3:00 and all planes bore evidence of flak. It was dusk as the last plane landed, signaling the end of the day. Christmas Night, and empty beds filled the tents. No one reveled or rejoiced in wild abandon. Thoughts were with those men "somewhere out there." The results on the last mission were undetermined, with no photos taken due to the severe evasive action used. Another of our aircraft was forced down, piloted by a crew from the 669th. The crew reported later, safe and sound. The curtain fell on Christmas of "44." It is better to leave words unspoken.[6]

*668th Bombardment Squadron (L) History.* Transcription from USAF Archives

Christmas 1944 proved, ironically enough, the most disastrous day in the Squadron's history. Through cloudless skies, our aircraft participated in two highly successful missions against supply points behind the Ardennes salient. Intense accurate hostile ground fire was encountered on both sorties. The following personnel failed to return and are missing in action: Capt. Richard V. Miracle, Capt. Richard B. Prentiss, 1st Lt. Jack J. Burg, 1st Lt. Francis H. Bursiel, 1st Lt. Robert R. Svenson, S/Sgt. Daniel M. Brown, S/Sgt. Arthur F. Galloway, S/Sgt. Phillip G. Fild, S/Sgt. John R. Simmonds and Sgt. Alvin C. Wylie.

Captains Miracle and Prentiss were original combat pilots of the Squadron. Captain Miracle, West Point graduate of the class of '42, was an able and respected officer on the threshold of a promising military career. Captain Prentiss, veteran of many hours of antisubmarine patrol in the Caribbean, and was a Flight Commander whose professional skill and wide experience will be sorely missed. Lieutenants Burg and Bursiel had both outstanding records as bombardiers, and they, as well as Lt. Svenson, were nearing the completion of their operational tours. S/Sgt. Fild was on the last mission of his combat tour.[7]

---

*"When You Go Home, Tell Them of Us and Say,*
*For Your Tomorrow, We Gave Our Today."*

*~ John Maxwell Edmonds*

---

# PRIVATE FIRST CLASS
# ROYAL R. ROGERS

*7th Field Artillery Battalion, 1st Division*
*DOW October 24, 1944*
*Medals: Purple Heart*
*Serial # 11015650*
*Plot F Row 15 Grave 74*

The birth of their son, Royal Rufus, on September 11, 1918, brought reason to celebrate for new parents, Harry and Marion (Chapman) Rogers, of Johnson, Vermont.[1] Known as Rufus, he became a sibling to Harold, Nancy, and Peter. Brother Peter remembers Rufus as a good-natured, hard-working, and strong individual. He also possessed a friendly, smiley countenance.[2]

Rufus completed grammar school and worked on the family dairy farm. "He was the quintessential all-American farm boy."[3] His

(Photo courtesy of Peter Rogers.)

brother, Peter, continues, "Rufus was to have taken over the family farm. Our parents were so disheartened by his being killed that they sold the farm."[4] Cousins Graydon and Bob recount the following memory of life on the farm with Rufus:

> In the pasture behind the barn was a steep sand bank that we, Graydon and Bob, liked to jump in. Also in the pasture was Pedro the Jersey bull. Pedro took issue with us invading his territory so he roared, pawed, and charged. We climbed a tree and Pedro took up residence below us. Rufus watched the whole thing and, seventy-four years later, we can still envision him leaning against the barn door with a big smile on his face, hollering up to us, "What are you two boy sprouts going to do now?"[5]

Rufus answered the call to serve and entered the military on October 12, 1940, one month after his twenty-second birthday.[6] He and Shirley Patch (paternal cousin of PFC Howard D. Lapan; Shirley's father, Mark, and Howard Lapan's mother, Eliza, were siblings[7]) of Johnson, Vermont, married on July 16, 1942.[8] Together they had one child, a son named Larry, who was born on February 5, 1943.[9] Father and son never met. PFC Royal Rogers, the man with an infectious smile who loved farming, who was to inherit the family farm and perhaps one day pass it along to his son, never had the opportunity to do so. He deployed to Europe and served with the 7th Field Artillery Battalion of the 1st Division. He was wounded in action on October 15, 1944, in Germany and died of wounds on October 24, 1944, in Belgium, four years after entering the military.[10] From Peter Rogers: "Rufus never got to see his son Larry. He gave me, his kid brother Peter, permission to use his 16-gauge shotgun while he was gone. I was twelve when he was killed."[11]

PFC Roger's commanding officer wrote the following letter to Shirley Rogers, dated December 6, 1944, commending her husband as a hero and as a soldier:

Mrs Shirley P. Rogers
Johnson, Vermont

Dear Mrs Rogers:

                This letter is written to extend the sincerest sympathy
of myself and all men of my organization on the death of your husband
Pfc Royal R. Rogers, 11015650, who died of wounds in Belgium on
24 October 1944 from wounds received in Germany on 15 October 1944.

                Your husband was buried in Belgium where a Protestant
Chaplain officiated at the burial.

                I have personally known Pfc Rogers for over 2 years
4 months as a member of Battery A. He was a superior soldier, admired

Dear Mrs. Rogers,

This letter is written to extend the sincerest sympathy of myself and all men of my organization on the death of your husband PFC Royal R. Rogers, 11015650, who died of wounds in Belgium on 24 October 1944, from wounds received in Germany on 15 October 1944.

Your husband was buried in Belgium where a Protestant Chaplain officiated at the burial.

I have personally known PFC Rogers for over 2 years 4 months as a member of Battery A. He was a superior soldier, admired and respected by all officers and men of the Battery for his courage, efficiency, and loyalty. His conduct and character throughout his service was exemplary and his loss will be keenly felt both as a soldier and as a friend.

Royal's duty in action was driver. He performed his duty in a superior manner under the most difficult combat conditions. He proved himself capable of performing assignments given only to the most trustworthy and efficient men.

All the officers and men of this Battery have requested that I speak for them and tell you how proud they are to have known and been associated with PFC Rogers.

Sincerely yours,
R.J. Nelson
Capt 7th FA Bn
Commanding Btry A[12]

(Photo courtesy of Peter Rogers.)

On February 1, 1945, Shirley Rogers wrote a letter to the Army Effects Bureau, notifying the department that she had not yet received her husband's personal belongings. She concluded her request with the following statement, "I want these for our little son to have because they belonged to his father."[13] At the time of his death, PFC Rogers possessed the usual items, which included souvenir coins, a wallet, letters, and a pen. He also possessed a photo book which contained twenty-six photos of family.[14]

PFC Roger's mother-in-law and Larry's legal guardian, Katherine Patch, contacted the Adjutant General Office in February 1949, inquiring to the burial location of her son-in-law and grandson's father. In the letter she writes, "Larry is six years old. The age when children ask questions and expect honest answers."[15] Larry, the son who never met his father, passed away in 2002.[16] Though it will never be known if his questions received honest answers, the fact is that his father died in service to others and is greatly respected as well as remembered by descendants of those he helped to liberate.

---

*"War has been waged against us by stealth and deceit and murder. This nation is peaceful, but fierce when stirred to anger. This conflict was begun on the timing and terms of others. It will end in a way, and at an hour, of our choosing."*

*~ George W. Bush*

---

# PRIVATE
# DURWARD W. ROLLINS

*346ᵗʰ Infantry Regiment, 87ᵗʰ Division*
*KIA January 8, 1945*
*Medals: Purple Heart*
*Serial # 31403150*
*Plot F Row 12 Grave 67*

Theodore Roosevelt was president of the United States when Durward Warner Rollins was born on June 19, 1908, in Hardwick, Vermont.[1] His parents were Claude and Sadie (Warner) Rollins.[2] Brother Lloyd arrived two years later.[3] Durward completed two years of high school and also worked on the family farm.[4]

He and Irene Kingsley, of Windsor, Vermont, married on October 23, 1935.[5] Together they had one child, Rhoda Irene, who was born on June 2, 1944.[6] At the time of his daughter's birth, Private Rollins had been in the military for seven months. The couple had resided in Goshen and Brandon, Vermont. Irene Rollins received notification in a telegram from the War Department dated January 30, 1945, that her husband had been listed as missing in action on January 8, 1945. She then received another notification in February that her husband's status had been changed to killed in action on January 8,

1945, in Bastogne, Belgium.[7] Irene also had received notification that her husband had been killed in France, prompting her to write the following letter to the Quartermaster General dated August 1, 1945:

Dear Sir:

It is in a very confused state of mind that I am writing you for any information you may be able to give me.

My husband, PVT Durward W. Rollins, ASN 31403150, was killed in action 8 January, 1945. Sometime ago, I received a letter from Brig. General Frank L. Culin, Jr. telling me that he was killed at Bastogne, Belgium (in the 87th Infantry) with burial in Belgium. Now I am in receipt of a letter from Chaplain Frank R. Mouer saying that he was with the 346th Infantry and was killed near Tillet, Belgium, in the advance on that town, with burial in U.S. Military Cemetery #1 Grand Failly, France.

Can you clarify information as to who may be right?

To date I have never received any personal effects. Could you tell me if there were any returned and where they might be?

Thanking You.

Irene B. Rollins[8]

She received the following reply a month later:

Dear Mrs. Rollins,

Acknowledgement is made of your letter requesting information concerning your husband, the late Private Durward W. Rollins.

The official report of interment received in this office shows that the remains of your husband were interred at United States Military Cemetery, Foy, Belgium, Plot A, Row 3, Grave 58. With reference to larger cities the appropriate location of Foy,

Belgium is four miles northeast of Bastogne and twenty miles southeast of Marche, both in Belgium.

In view of the fact that the Army Effects Bureau, Kansas City Quartermaster Depot, Kansas City 1, Missouri, has been designated to receive and ship the personal effects of our military personnel who have died outside the United States, a copy of your letter has been forwarded to that office for a direct reply to you.

This office regrets, sincerely, the delay in answering your letter and wishes to extend its deepest sympathy in the loss of your husband.[9]

The *Burlington Free Press* published an announcement on March 10, 1945, for PVT Rollins:

Brandon- A military mass will be celebrated Monday at 8:30 at the Church of Our Lady of Good Help by Rev. Mark J. Harvey for Private Durward W. Rollins, 36, killed in action Jan. 8 in Belgium.

His widow received notice of his death on Feb. 26, but she had previously been advised by the war department that her husband was missing on Jan. 8. Both messages were confirmed.

Private Rollins was born in Hardwick, June 19, 1908, son of the late Claude and Sadie (Warner) Rollins. On October 23, 1935, he married Miss Irene Kingsley of Windsor. After living in Hardwick, he lived in Brandon and when he entered the service in Dec., 1943, he was operating a farm in Goshen, where his wife and nine months old daughter are living.

Private Rollins trained at the Aberdeen, Md., Proving Grounds and went to England in Aug. last year, remaining there until Thanksgiving time, when he was transferred from ordnance to the infantry and sent to France.

31 December 1948

Pvt Durward W. Rollins, ASN 31 403 150
Plot F, Row 12, Grave 67
Headstone: Cross
Henri-Chapelle U. S. Military Cemetery

Mrs. Irene B. Rollins
Box 72
Brandon, Vermont

Dear Mrs. Rollins:

This is to inform you that the remains of your loved one have been permanently interred, as recorded above, side by side with comrades who also gave their lives for their country. Customary military funeral services were conducted over the grave at the time of burial.

After the Department of the Army has completed all final interments, the cemetery will be transferred, as authorized by the Congress, to the care and supervision of the American Battle Monuments Commission. The Commission also will have the responsibility for permanent construction and beautification of the cemetery, including erection of the permanent headstone. The headstone will be inscribed with the name exactly as recorded above, the rank or rating where appropriate, organization, State, and date of death. Any inquiries relative to the type of headstone or the spelling of the name to be inscribed thereon, should be addressed to the American Battle Monuments Commission, the central address of which is Room 713, 1712 "G" Street, N. W., Washington 25, D. C. Your letter should include the full name, rank, serial number, grave location, and name of the cemetery.

While interment activities are in progress, the cemetery will not be open to visitors. However, upon completion thereof, due notice will be carried by the press.

You may rest assured that this final interment was conducted with fitting dignity and solemnity and that the grave-site will be carefully and conscientiously maintained in perpetuity by the United States Government.

Sincerely yours,

THOMAS B. LARKIN
Major General
The Quartermaster General

lho

Besides his wife and daughter he is survived by his mother, who is now Mrs. John Edgar of Brandon, and a brother, Sgt. Lloyd Rollins, with the Marines.[10]

---

*"Is life so dear or peace so sweet as to be purchased at the price of chains and slavery? Forbid it, Almighty God! I know not what course others may take, but as for me, give me liberty, or give me death!"*

*~ Patrick Henry*

---

# PRIVATE
# THOMAS H. SORRELL

*506ᵗʰ Parachute Infantry Regiment, 101ˢᵗ Airborne Division*
*KIA December 19, 1944*
*Medals: Good Conduct, WWII Victory,*
*EAME Campaign, Bronze Star, Purple Heart*
*Serial #31340558*
*Plot E Row 16 Grave 52*

Tom's personal history, written by nephew James Sorrell:

Thomas Henry Sorrell was born on July 23, 1925, in Fairfield, Vermont. Tom was the third of eight children born to Leo George and Vatleana Furkey Sorrell. A child of the Depression, Tom grew up during hard times. These were times when he took the initiative to seek donations of day-old bread from the local bakery for his family, and times when he was so embarrassed by his frayed

Pvt. Thomas Henry Sorrell - Late 1943

(Photo courtesy of James Sorrell.)

shoelaces that he asked the clerk in the local shoe store for polish that he might use to mask their condition and avoid the teasing of his classmates.

Tom completed school through the 8th grade and the summer just before he turned fourteen years old, he went to work as a hand on a dairy farm in order to be self-supporting and to contribute to the family. He was known in the family as a practical joker, ever ready to hatch a plot to ensnare a friend or family member, to the amusement of all. Tom was a fun-loving, outgoing, and adventurous young man.

Like many men of his generation across the country, he longed to see and experience the world beyond the rural setting in which he'd been raised. This restless and adventurous spirit prompted Tom to join the army on his first day of eligibility on July 26, 1943. He had just turned eighteen years old on the previous Friday and no longer required his mother's permission to enlist. Her permission had been consistently denied and now he was free to act on his own behalf.

Tom's military career began with Basic Training as a part of the US Army 63$^{rd}$ Infantry Division based at Camp Van Dorn in Centreville, Mississippi.

Upon completion of basic and further training as a truck driver it appears that Tom received orders for overseas deployment via Camp Meade, Maryland. Having never been away from family and friends for such an extended time, Tom longed to go home before being sent overseas. Without benefit of the approval of his superiors, he took leave for two weeks. To put it more directly, he went absent without leave (AWOL) for two weeks by hitchhiking back to Vermont, proving again that he was just the take-charge kind of guy we needed to pit against the German army.

Thomas H. Sorrell

Sunday Mail Call - Mid Dec. 1943, Camp Van Dorn, MS

(Photo courtesy of James Sorrell.)

Prior to returning to his base, he confided to family members that he didn't believe he would be returning from Europe. This premonition unfortunately came to pass.

After paying for his misdeeds with a stint on Kitchen Patrol (KP), Tom volunteered for the Airborne in the Parachute Infantry. Apparently, he was tempted by the additional 50 dollars a month hazardous duty pay and the thought of not being stuck behind the steering wheel of a truck. It is believed that he completed Airborne training at Fort Benning, Georgia in early 1944.

He then shipped out for additional training in England prior to ultimately being placed into action on the mainland of Europe. As he didn't go into Airborne training until the winter of '44, he was far behind the training schedule of the D-Day troops. During the summer months following D-Day (June '44), he experienced the illness, surgery, and recovery associated with an appendectomy. While in recovery, he wrote home to his mother to communicate his condition. The heading of that letter indicated that he was a member of the 506th Parachute Infantry Regiment of the 101st Airborne.

The transcription of that letter reads as follows:

"Dear Mother,

How is everybody getting along? I suppose it's pretty hot out there now. I went out to a little carnival and had a pretty good time. When did you see Leon last? I suppose he is pretty busy right now. My side is pretty well healed up now. It don't bother me anymore but I lost about 12 lbs. I have it pretty easy here, just lay all day in bed and write letters and shoot the bull. How is John getting along down at the bakery? And, how is Estella coming along? Tell Estella to tell Ann, I would write her today but I'm lazy so Estella can give her my love, ha! ha! I don't know what to write so I will say so long to you all. Good luck, Your Son, Pvt. Sorrell"

Further, it is believed that after the Allied losses of the Market Garden offensive of September in Holland, Tom was called into action as part of the move to refresh the ranks of the 506th. On December 16th of '44, the German army began a counterattack pushing westward across the Ardenne Forest of Belgium and the Battle of the Bulge was underway. General Eisenhower called upon the 101st Airborne to slow the German army push until General Patton's Army could engage and repeal the advance.

On Dec. 19th the 101st Airborne arrived from Mourmelon, France via trucks to the vicinity of Bastogne, Belgium, with the mission to deny German Panzer's access to the roads west out of Bastogne. Tom was among the troopers in H Company of the 506th Parachute Infantry

Regiment positioned to engage the enemy on that day. In the late afternoon of the 19th, Tom lost his life by sustaining severe wounds to his head and abdomen. At the age of nineteen, his life was given in service to his comrades, his family and his country. Tom fell at a location just outside of Foy, Belgium, some 3.5 miles north of Bastogne.

Due to the fog of war, Tom's reported status went from Severely Wounded In Action (SWA) to Missing in Action (MIA) to Killed In Action (KIA) over a six-month period. Tom thought of his family by securing a life insurance policy in his mother's name before he went into combat. That policy paid out a monthly stipend from the time of his death until the time of hers. In addition, specific jump and glider pay amounts were also sent home, further demonstrating his continuing dedication to his family.

Tom was one of more than 400,000 Americans to give themselves to a great struggle against a tyranny and injustice known to history as World War II. He was a young US Army Private from a rural state who had seen little of the world before he enlisted. Within a few months of that enlistment, he found himself at the center of major world-changing events. He had courageously volunteered for hazardous duty as a parachute infantryman with the 101st

# 5 Local GI's Backed 'Nuts!' Of McAuliffe

Five boys from this section are members of the 506th parachute infantry regiment which backed up the "Nuts!" first ejaculated by Brig.-Gen. Anthony C. McAuliffe, acting commander of the 101st Airborne Division, and since cracked around the world.

This decisive bit of slang was the general's answer to the German demand for surrender when the Yanks were sealed in Bastogne shortly after the start of the Battle of the Bulge.

Pvt. Thomas H. Sorrell of Burlington, Pvt. Othello B. Davis, Essex Junction, Corp. Jules M. Chicoine and S/Sgt. Henry J. Rocheleau, St. Albans and Sgt. Donald A. Baron of Winooski were among those who attacked continuously until a corridor had been established with our own troops.

In addition to participating in the battle of Bastogne, the 506th played a major role in the success of the Normandy and Holland campaigns. It took part in the fall of Carentan and later liberated Eindhoven in Holland. It twice took the measure of the elite German Sixth Parachute Regiment in attaining victories in France and Holland.

Clipping from the Burlington Free Press Newspaper - Battle of The Bulge

(Photo courtesy of James Sorrell.)

# Pvt. Sorrell Now Listed As Dead

The War Department has finally given up for lost Pvt. Thomas H. Sorrell, 19-year-old paratrooper son of Mr. and Mrs. Leo Sorrell of 4 Bellevue Street, Winooski.

In winter action in Belgium Dec. 19 the soldier was reported missing, but Wednesday the final word came from headquarters. Private Sorrell was with the 506th Parachute Infantry Regiment.

Besides his parents he is survived by four sisters, Mrs. Marion Trombley, Colchester, Mrs. Estella Trombley, Glenna and Helen Sorrell of Winooski; two brothers, Leon of North Hero and John of Winooski, and by one nephew, Leon Trombley.

Private Sorrell was born in Private Sorrell was born in at\ended South Burlington school. He trained at Camp Van Dorn, Miss., and Camp Meade, Md.

Clipping from the Burlington
Free Press Newspaper

(Photo courtesy of James Sorrell.)

Airborne Division during a time of raging war. His courage made him an active participant in these events and an instrument for the defeat of a great evil.[1]

Extended effects of Tom's Loss – A Family Postscript:

I can recall, as a child, looking at Tom's portrait on my grandparents' living room wall and wondering who he was and why we didn't talk about him. All I knew was that he was an uncle "killed in the war." His loss was so painful and the family grief so deep that we had to suppress any thoughts of him, lest we would be overcome. My elderly father could not speak of Tom without breaking down in tears. That's how unprocessed the family's grief was, and how close to the surface the pain had remained for decades.

There had been no grief counseling. You just had to suck it up and get on with your life, but the remnants of that unresolved pain filtered into the experience of each of our lives. Each of us of the next generation was affected to varying degrees by Tom's loss. Our parents, Tom's brothers and sisters, were never helped to understand that Tom lived a beautiful and loving, if short, life that should have been honored and celebrated instead of buried in grief. The last thing that Tom would have wanted was to inflict suffering on those he loved. In that sense, we of his family have unknowingly failed him.

Many of us from the next generation are well into our sixties and even the youngest of us are AARP eligible. It's my hope that knowing more of Tom's story will help us all appreciate and honor his fun loving, adventurous, brave and loving spirit. And further, that we will proudly share his story with our children and grandchildren.[2]

On February 7, 1945, PFC Olson of 3043d QM Gr. Reg. Co. evacuated the bodies of eight soldiers to U.S. Military Cemetery #1, Foy, Belgium.[3] Among these men were two unidentified soldiers, Unknown X-6 and Unknown X-43. They and the other six soldiers were interred at the military cemetery on February 17, 1945.[4] From the Report of Burial for Unknown X-43 dated 7 March 45:

> Report of Burial for Unknown X-43, who died as result of SW head and abdomen, 25 Jan 45, est., Foy, Belgium. Buried 17 Feb 45 in the US Military Cemetery #1, Foy, Belgium, Plot F, Row 3, Grave 65. The body was badly decomposed, but fingerprints were taken of the first three fingers of the left hand. The deceased was estimated to be 6'0" tall; weighed 175 lbs.; medium build and fair complexion. The hair is short and straight. Nose is long and sharp and the ears are large. The jaw is square, and the fingernails are short and square cut. There is a 3" scar from an old appendectomy. The following information taken from the effects found on the remains:
>
> > A girl's snapshot on the back which was written, "To Pvt. ------- --------, 506 Paratroop Inf. APO 412 from Anita La Mott, Grand Falls, Vt" seems to be the best clue as to the identity of this man. The name has been scratched out with pen or indelible pencil.
> >
> > A Xmas card from "your loving sister, Estella" another

is signed Rev JB McGarry, and another "From Mother" and one that is signed "Grace D" shows a photo of a girl in a GI blouse with T/5 chevrons.

A slip of paper headed: "M R Hqs-Reading" with the message: "Pick up Pvt. Specci and any other prisoners there" and signed by Lt. M M Miller P&P Officer 506 PI was also found.[5]

Personnel with the Quartermaster General's Office called Father Collins at St. Anne's Church, "requesting the address of Rev JB McGarry, probably a pastor of a church in Vermont."[6] Rev. John B. McGarry was indeed a pastor at St. Stephen's Church located in Winooski, VT. The Quartermaster General's Office issued the following letter to him dated 17 April 45:

Dear Father McGarry:

An attempt is being made by this office to identify the remains of an Unknown Deceased, killed in Belgium during January.

Among the personal effects was found a Christmas card signed: "Rev J.B. McGarry"; one from "your loving sister Estella", and one from his mother.

The deceased was believed to have been a member of the 506th Paratroop Infantry.

It is requested that any information you may possess, relative to the identity of this soldier, be forwarded to this office at the earliest practicable date. It is also requested that this matter be treated confidentially.

A franked envelope, which requires no additional postage, is enclosed for your convenience.

For the Quartermaster General:

Sincerely yours,
Mayo A. Darling[7]

Rev. John B. McGarry issued the following reply on April 29, 1945, one day before Adolf Hitler committed suicide in Berlin, Germany:

Dear Sir:

Re: To your communication of the seventeenth inst. regarding identity of unknown deceased.

According to your letter, a Christmas card from me, one signed, "your loving sister, Estella," and one from his mother was found on the body.

I have had an interview with Mrs. Estella Trombley, a sister of Thomas H. Sorrell, 6 Bellevue Street, Winooski. She tells me her brother, Thomas H. Sorrell, enlisted in the army July 23, 1943. At that time he was living with his mother at 62 Dorset Street, South Burlington, Vermont.

The last letter the family received from him was dated December 17, 1944. She tells me that at that time he was with the Paratroop Infantry in Belgium. She showed me three wires from the War Department to his mother, Mrs. Vetlina Sorrell, dated January 16, March 25, and April 17, 1945. The last wire stated that he had been missing in action since December 1944, and that he had previously been wounded in action.

According to your letter and the testimony of Mrs. Estella Trombley, no doubt the unknown deceased is no other than Thomas H. Sorrell. I didn't tell Mrs. Trombley that I had received a communication from the War Department regarding her brother.

If I can be of any further service to the War Department in this case, I will gladly do so.

Sincerely yours,
John B. McGarry[8]

The quest to properly identify Unknown X-43 continued with a letter dated 4 May 1945, from the Commanding General of the Third United States Army to the Commanding Officer of the 4117 U.S. Army Hospital Plant:

1. An unidentified soldier was buried in U.S. Military Cemetery No. 1, Foy, Belgium on 17 February 1945, as Unknown X-43. His body was recovered in the vicinity of Foy, Belgium, at the same time and in the same area as the bodies of Jack J. Walsh, Joseph S. Baker, Leonard E. Lundquist, Roy F. Stuart, Robert W. Kangas, and Martin E. Mize were recovered. The only clothing marking found was the name "Woolcot" on a web belt. The following personal effects were found on the remains:

A Christmas card signed "Grace D." showing a picture of a girl wearing a blouse, wool, OD, with Tec 5 chevrons
A Christmas card signed, "Rev. J.B. McGarry."
A Christmas card to "Our Boy" from "Mother."
A religious Christmas card signed, "Your loving sister Estella"
A blank QMC Form No. 424 (Stock Record)
A small ruled note book about 2.5 x 4 inches
A Unit Citation Ribbon
A safety razor
A piece of paper headed, "MR Hqs-Reading" with message, "Pick up Pvt. Specci and any other prisoners there," signed "Lt. M M Miller, P&P Officer."

2. It has been reported that Lt. Miller is a patient in the 4117 U.S. Army Hospital Plant. If he is available for questioning, it is requested that he furnish answers to the following questions:

 a. What is the name of the man who was carrying the message signed by him?

 b. Can he recognize the description of Unknown X-43 which is contained in the attached report of burial as being similar to that of a former member of the 506th Parachute Infantry Regiment? If so, what is the man's name?

 c. Can Lt. Miller discover any clue from the description of the personal effects listed above which might aid in identifying the deceased soldier?

3. If Lt. Miller is no longer in the 4117th Hospital Plant, it is requested that this correspondence be forwarded to his present address.[9]

Lt. Miller was unable to remember the identity of Unknown X-43 and provide any further assistance.[10]

Based upon Rev. McGarry's response letter stating the unknown deceased "is no other than Thomas H. Sorrell", personnel from the Office of the Quartermaster General submitted the fingerprints of Unknown X-43 to the FBI for comparison with the prints of Thomas H. Sorrell on May 5, 1945.[11] One week later, Unknown X-43 gained a name: that of Thomas H. Sorrell, the same person who had been born nineteen years prior at the family home in Fairfield, Vermont. His grandmother delivered him as she had with his siblings.[12] "He was very outgoing and full of fun when he went to war," remembers his youngest sister, Helen Sorrell Siple. She continues, "He told my mother he would never be back. He was very brave and loving."[13]

From nephew James Sorrell:

Why is it important for the Sorrell family to think about, to talk about, to honor and to document Tom's service? This service was not only to his country in a distant or vague sense. It was also to each of us in his family that has benefited from the freedoms and opportunities that his sacrifice helped to secure. Each one of us, though we honestly have a tendency to take it all for granted, has lived very blessed lives. We owe a great debt to Tom. He faced fear and hatred in the form of artillery, tank, machine gun, and rifle fire so that we wouldn't have to.

How do we repay even a portion of this debt? The short answer is by remembering. We must have the courage to not sadly but to gratefully, proudly, and lovingly remember, for in our memory he still lives. Our memories provide a here and now link to his eternal spirit. If we forget him or fail to document his legacy through this record, not only are we abandoning him, but we are blocking future generations of this family from knowing and honoring his spirit. He didn't fail us and we can't fail to remember and appreciate him.[14]

Sister Helen Sorrell Siple shares the following memory:

Tom gave me $.50 to buy candy when he was home on leave. He put it on the counter and said, "Take it to put away before Pa takes it." I did and bought candy. Ever since, I wished I kept it for a memory of him. Of course at eleven years old I never dreamed he would get killed. To this day I never could figure out why no one in the family would ever talk about him. I guess it is a mystery that I will never understand. I was so young, but used to sit around and tried to figure it out. I loved him dearly and would have given my life for him. God Bless him.[15]

She continues, "I played the guitar and made up a song about Tom to sing to all my brothers and sisters in the room. They all left as no one wanted to talk about him except my mother. She never acted the same since he was killed. My mother cried a lot and she also mentioned his name often."[16]

Helen's song about Tom:

*Death of Brother Tom*

*I didn't think it was right*
*When Tom went off to fight*
*Such a handsome and young man was he*
*His blond hair and blue eyes took everyone's eyes.*

*If for everyone's sake, the world wouldn't be full of hate*
*How I wished it could be that Tom could be here today.*
*The news was hard to bear that Tom should die*
*a hero over there.*
*A smaller family are we all because of the death of Brother Tom.*

*Tom died in World War Two*
*Went off to fight for me and you!*
*His smiling face I'll always see*
*As he died for the freedom of his own*
*Beloved home of so far away.*
*I'm sure that God watches over Brother Tom*
*And this country so dear to you and me![17]*

"I know he was very brave. I want people to remember and to keep him in their prayers always because he was a great hero and loved by all. I never will forget him and I pray for him daily."[18] A devoted sister's wish and action for her brother, a member of the Greatest Generation, who selflessly offered his life for those same people that Helen Sorrell Siple hopes will remember and honor him.

In the words of nephew James Sorrell, "This young man that went up against German Panzer Tanks with just an M1 rifle in his hand, deserves not only our respect, but also to be remembered openly with gratitude."[19] In service of that objective, the following letter was mailed to all of the surviving members of the Leo and Vatleana Sorrell Family line, down to the grandchildren, prior to the day marking the 70th year from Tom's loss.

---

December 7, 2014

Subject: Thomas Henry Sorrell Remembrance

Dear Grandparents, Parents & Children of the Sorrell Family,

You'll find enclosed a 5" x 7" print that commemorates the 70th year since the loss of Pvt. Thomas Henry Sorrell during the Battle of the Bulge in Foy, Belgium, on Dec. 19, 1944. I'm encouraging you to take a moment on the upcoming Dec. 19th to think about Tom's life and legacy.

Tom was a fun loving, adventurous 19 year old young man, but his memory has been shrouded in a deep and painful grief for many decades. I'd like us to celebrate his courageous well lived life. He loved to joke and laugh. He apparently had an eye for the girls, which a number of us can appreciate. However, beyond that he had a good and generous heart. His nature was sharing and supportive, and these characteristics reveal a loving if sometimes, boisterous soul. It was these aspects of his nature that led him on the hero's journey.

How was this young Vermont farm boy a hero? He enlisted in the United States Army in the middle of the terrors of WWII. He volunteered for hazardous duty in the Airborne while sending money home to contribute to the support of his family. And, he gave his life in support of the mission but most telling, I believe, in support of his fellow troopers on the ground and in the action that day. I'm using the word 'support' here to be synonymous with 'an extension of love'.

So, Tom is a heroic, not a tragic figure in our family. He really did lead a beautiful and loving life that we should honor and celebrate by taking a few minutes to remember him on occasions like this 70th year milestone. I further encourage you to share Tom's story with your children and grandchildren so that the awareness of his life and contributions will live on after us.

Thank you for your time and attention to this message.

In extension of Tom's love,
Jim

---

BECAUSE YOU EARNED YOUR
WINGS, WE'VE BEEN FREE TO
FLY. WITH GRATITUDE, PRIDE
AND LOVE FROM YOUR FAMILY
ON THIS 60TH ANNIVERSARY
OF YOUR SACRIFICE.

WE REMEMBER -
DECEMBER 19, 2004

ONE OF THE
SCREAMING EAGLES
506TH REGIMENT
101ST AIRBORNE

AIRBORNE

THOMAS H. SORRELL
JULY 23, 1925 - DECEMBER 19, 1944

70 years ago today you gave your life in the line of duty, in defense of freedom, at Foy, Belgium, during the Battle of the Bulge. At 19 years old, you demonstrated great bravery in support of a perilous mission. The pain of your loss is still felt. However, we've always taken solace in the knowledge that brave young men like you helped to advance humanity in the face of great inhumanity. You fell in war, but rest in peace with 8,000 of your Brothers in Arms at the Henri-Chapelle American Cemetery in Belgium. Time has only enhanced our gratitude for your legacy and appreciation of your sacrifice.

Signed: Family and Friends[20]

---

*"We fight not to enslave, but to set a country free, and to make room upon the earth for honest men to live in."*

*~ Thomas Paine*

---

# PRIVATE
# LOGAN E. WARNER

*505th Parachute Infantry Regiment, 82nd Airborne Division*
*KIA December 21, 1944*
*Medals: Purple Heart*
*Serial # 31046354*
*Plot F Row 10 Grave 20*

Logan Edwin Warner was born on July 28, 1922, in Ludlow, Vermont.[1] His parents were Logan and Lillian (Alaire) and Gertrude and Eleanor were his two older sisters. Both Gertrude and Eleanor were deceased at the time of Logan's birth. Logan became an older brother to Mary and eventually to Natalie.[2]

"Bud", as he was known, completed one year of high school and worked as a machinist in Windsor, Vermont.[3] Sister Natalie Warner Gruber remembers that he was well-liked by all who met and knew him. "In school, the girls would always come to the house and try to get

(Photo courtesy of Natalie Warner Gruber.)

him to go to the junior prom with them, but he never did. I took his death harder than anyone. We were very close. I couldn't mention his name without crying for over a year."[4] She continues,

> Bud got a leave he didn't know was coming and got home early one afternoon. I was in school. He couldn't wait to see me so started down the road. We saw each other at the same time and started running. He picked me up in his arms.
> One night we had a cake with frosting for dessert. Mary (our sister) put all of her frosting on a fork and said, "Who wants my frosting?" Bud said, "I do," and grabbed it, eating all the frosting. Boy was she mad!
> I cried when he left after his last leave. He said, "Don't cry. I'll be back." It was not to be.[5]

Logan "Bud" entered the military on August 5, 1941, as a single man with no dependents.[6] He was later stationed at Fort Adams, Rhode Island, where he married Flora Dupont, who resided in Middleton, Rhode Island.[7] "He never saw her again after leaving Rhode Island for Texas."[8] Private Warner served with the 505th Parachute Infantry Regiment, 82nd Airborne Division and was initially classified as missing in action on December 21, 1944, only to be determined as killed in action on December 21, 1944, in Wanne, Belgium.[9] Readers of the *Springfield Reporter* learned of PVT Warner's death on February 1, 1945:

### Logan E. Warner Killed in Action

Ludlow- The name of Logan E. Warner, 22, paratrooper, is another name to be added to Ludlow heroes killed or missing in action as the word was received Wednesday, Jan. 17, by his parents, Mr. and Mrs. Logan S. Warner, that he was reported missing in action in Belgium Dec. 21.

Pvt. Warner enlisted [ ] and was sent to Fort Eutis, Va., and later was at Fort Adams, Newport, R.I., and at Fort Bliss,

Texas, until May 1944, and then studied Radar at Camp McCoy, Wis., until he went overseas in September 1944.

He was at a paratrooper school in England for six weeks and then was sent to France and Belgium where he apparently saw a large amount of action up to December 1944.

Pvt. Warner was another of Ludlow's popular young men who wanted to do his part in winning the war...[10]

Natalie Warner Gruber wants her brother to be remembered and known for being a "loved and kind person."[11]

## Logan E. Warner Killed In Action

LUDLOW — The name of Logan E. Warner, 22, paratrooper, is another name to be added to Ludlow heroes killed or missing in action as word was received Wednesday, Jan. 17, by his parents, Mr. and Mrs. Logan S. Warner that he was reported missing in action in Belgium Dec. 21.

Pvt. Warner enlisted August 4, 1942, and was sent to Fort Eutis, Va., and later was at Fort Adams, Newport, R. I., and at Fort Bliss, Texas, until May 1944, and then studied Radar at Camp McCoy, Wis., until he went overseas in September 1944.

He was at a paratrooper school in England for six weeks and then was sent to France and Belgium where he apparently saw a large amount of action up to December 1944.

Pvt. Warner was another of Ludlow's popular young men who wanted to do his part in winning the war and enlisted in 1942. The surviving relatives are his parents, his wife living in Newport, N. H., and sisters, the Misses Mary and Natalie, living at home.

*"I believe our flag is more than just cloth and ink. It is a universally recognized symbol that stands for liberty, and freedom. It is the history of our nation, and it's marked by the blood of those who died defending it."*

*~ John Thune*

# PRIVATE FIRST CLASS
# GARTH A. WHITTIER

*23th Infantry Regiment, 2nd Division*
*KIA January 20, 1945*
*Medals: Purple Heart*
*Serial # 31339873*
*Plot F Row 7 Grave 27*

Calvin Coolidge was President of the United States and Benito Mussolini was dictator of Italy when Garth Whittier was born on January 12, 1925, in Cherry River, Quebec, Canada, to parents Lloyd and Addie (Meigs).[1] He had one older brother named Norman and would eventually become a brother to two younger sisters, Catherine and Shirley, who remember, "Our family moved to Newport, Vermont, when Garth was very young and lived in different parts of the state through the years."[2]

Garth enjoyed family and friends

(Photo courtesy of Shirley Whittier Holt. )

Dear Mr. Whittier:

The Army Effects Bureau has received from overseas
some more property of your son, Private First Class Garth
A. Whittier.

This property, contained in one package, is being
sent you for distribution. If, for some reason, it has not
been received within the next thirty days, this Bureau should
be informed so that tracer may be instituted.

Sincerely yours,

R. T. BROWN
1st Lt., QMC
Chief, Adm. Division

and liked to fish in the brook near the family's house. The friendly, quiet-mannered future soldier enjoyed dancing along with listening to music, although his biggest interest was reading.[3] He completed grammar school in Castleton, Vermont.

From sisters Catherine Whittier McKenney and Shirley Whittier Holt:

> Garth worked in the woods with our father for a short time, cutting trees for logs to be shipped to saw mills and processed into lumber. During this time, when he was eighteen, he received a notice from the draft board to be inducted into the service. He left soon after with a willing attitude as he wanted to serve his country. He left to go overseas a few months later.
>
> We looked forward to receiving letters from him as we know he did from us. Our mother made goodies to send him and other things he needed. We sent them in special cardboard boxes that were provided for this purpose. We listened on the radio often during the day to get the latest news about the war. It was constantly on our minds; very scary for everyone.
>
> It was a very sad time when we received news of his death. We couldn't believe it was true, but knew we had to accept it. There was a prayer service in our church for him with family

and friends. Our parents felt it was best to have him buried overseas. The family believed it was the right decision.

We will always miss him and believe we will see him again.[4]

Garth entered the military on May 31, 1943, and served with the 23rd Infantry Regiment, 2nd Division.[5] He was reported hospitalized on December 2, 1944, and included in a list of his personal effects were bathing trunks.[6] PFC Whittier was killed in action on January 20, 1945, in Faymonville, Belgium, eight days after his 20th birthday.[7]

---

*"These are the times that try men's souls. The summer soldier and the sunshine patriot will, in this crisis, shrink from the service of their county; but he that stands it now, deserves the love and thanks of man and woman. Tyranny like hell is not easily conquered; yet we have this consolation with us, the harder the conflict, the more glorious the triumph. What we obtain too cheap, we esteem too lightly; it is dearness only that gives everything its value."*

*~ Thomas Paine*

---

# APPENDIX I – MEDALS*

## Air Medal Recipients

"The **Air Medal**, established by Executive Order on 11 May 1942, and amended by Executive Order on 11 September 1942, is awarded to a person who, while serving with the United States Armed Forces, has distinguished himself or herself by meritorious achievement while participating in aerial flight. Awards may recognize single acts of heroism or merit, or may recognize sustained meritorious service over a period of six months or more. The Air Medal primarily recognizes personnel on flight status requiring frequent participation in aerial flight. It may be awarded to personnel not on flight status whose duties require frequent flight other than in a passenger status. The Air Medal ranks behind the Distinguished Flying Cross in order of precedence."

CAPT Richard Prentiss

## Bronze Star Recipients

"The **Bronze Star Medal** was established by an Executive Order of 4 February 1944, superseded by an Executive Order of 24 August amended by an Executive Order on 28 February 2003. It is awarded to a person who, while serving with or in the United States Army after 6 December 1941, distinguished himself or herself by heroic or meritorious achievement or service in connection with military operations against an armed enemy, or while engaged in military operations against an opposing armed force wherein the United States was not a belligerent party. Actions while in aerial flight are not covered by this award. Awards for acts of heroism rank immediately behind the Silver Star. Awards for acts of merit or meritorious service rank immediately behind the Legion of Merit. Provisions exist for retroactive awards covering the period 7 December 1941 through 1 July 1947, based upon citations in orders, related awards and certificates, and unit awards."

SSGT Arthur Jacobs
SGT Edward T. Jones Jr.
PVT Adelard Joyal
SSGT George Joyal
TEC 5 Raymond Muir

## Oak Leaf Cluster Recipients

"To denote the subsequent award of certain military awards." Authorized medals are: Defense Distinguished Service Medal, Silver Star, Defense Superior Service Medal, Legion of Merit (oak leaf clusters are not issued for the Legion of Merit in degrees to foreign nationals), Distinguished Flying Cross, Bronze Star, Purple Heart, Defense Meritorious Service Medal, Meritorious Service Medal, Joint Service Commendation Medal, Joint Service Achievement Medal, Presidential Unit Citation, and Joint Meritorious Unit Award."

SGT Norman Bishop
PFC Louis Connolly
PVT Harvey Colton Oliver
CAPT Richard Prentiss (9)

# Purple Heart Recipients

"The Purple Heart is awarded to members of the Armed Forces of the United States who after 5 April 1917, have been wounded or killed in action against an enemy of the United States or an opposing armed force, while serving with friendly foreign forces engaged in an armed conflict, as the result of acts of enemy or hostile opposing forces, as a result of terrorist attacks or attacks on peacekeeping forces since 28 March 1973, or by friendly fire in circumstance as described above."

PVT Leroy Baker
PVT Lawrence Bishop
SGT Norman Bishop
PFC John Carleton
PFC Claude Chapin
PFC Louis Connolly
PVT Gerard Desroches
PVT James Durkee
PVT Albert Gauthier
PFC Theodore Hall
SSGT Arthur Jacobs
SGT Edward Jones Jr.
PVT Adelard Joyal

SSGT George Joyal
PFC Howard Lapan
CPL Maurice Metivier
PFC Harold Mitchell
TEC 5 Raymond Muir
PVT Harvey Colton Oliver
PVT Maurice Ploof
PFC Royal Rogers
PVT Durward Rollins
PVT Thomas Sorrell
PVT Logan Warner
PFC Garth Whittier

# Silver Star Recipient

"The **Silver Star**, established by Act of Congress on 9 July 1918, and amended on 25 July 1963, is awarded to a person who, while serving in the United States Armed Forces, is cited for markedly distinct gallantry while in action against an enemy of the United States, while engaged in military operations involving conflict with an opposing or foreign force, or while serving with friendly foreign forces engaged in an armed conflict against an opposing armed force in which the United States is not a belligerent party. Upon application, it is awarded to individuals who received a citation for gallantry in published orders issued by a headquarters commanded by a general officer in World War I. In precedence for valor, the Silver Star ranks immediately behind the Distinguished Service Cross and the Navy Cross."

SSGT George Joyal

*Information taken from the American Battles Monument Commission website

# APPENDIX II – RESEARCH TOOLS

American Battle Monuments Commission: *www.abmc.gov*

Enlistment and other public records: *www.ancestry.com*, *www.familysearch.org*, www.nara.gov

Form letter to request a soldier's Individual Deceased Personnel File:

Date

Requester's Name and Address

U.S. Army Human Resources Command
Casualty & Memorial Affairs Operations Division
Attn: AHRC-PDC
1600 Spearhead Division Avenue Dept 450
Fort Knox, KY 40122-5405

Dear Sir or Madam,

I am requesting an Individual Deceased Personal File for (soldier's name) Serial #
During the war, he served in the (infantry regiment and division) and was KIA on (date).

Sincerely,


Name

E-mail address (will send electronically if e-mail address is provided.) How to request Official Military Personnel Files (OMPF). Free for veterans. Charge for any other individual, including next of kin.

Mail a letter or Standard Form (SF) 180 to:

National Personnel Records Center
1 Archives Drive
St. Louis, MO 63138

Necessary information to include in request: veteran's complete name as used in military, military identification number, branch of service, dates of service, date of birth, and place of birth. For records affected by the 1973 fire, include place of entry, last assigned unit, and place of discharge, if known.

Can also be requested online.

Visit: _http://www.archives.gov/st-louis/military-personnel/public/ general-public.html_ for more information.

How to request Morning Reports (there is a charge):

November 18, 2009

Requester's Name and Mailing Address
National Personnel Records Center
9700 Page Avenue
St. Louis, MO 63132

Dear Sir or Madam,

I am searching for records about my relative's service during WWII in the European Theatre of Operations, primarily unit operational records such as Morning Reports.
My relative, KIA, was name (Service Number #).
During this time he was in C Company, 78th Infantry Division of the 309th Infantry Regiment. He was KIA (date). I am requesting Morning Reports for the following:
Company C of 309th Infantry Regiment, 78th Infantry Division on the days of (dates of interest).
Any help you can provide is greatly appreciated.

Cordially,


Name


Phone:
Email:

How to request other reports:

Date

Requester's Name and Mailing Address
Modern Military Records (NWCTM)
National Archives at College Park
8601 Adelphi Road
College Park, MD 20740-6001

Dear Sir or Madam,

I am interested in obtaining copies of records from the Records of
the Adjunct General's Office (RG 407). I would like a price quote
for the following records of the 309th Infantry Regiment of the 78th
Infantry Division during WW2:

1) After Action Reports
2) Operation Journals
3) Overlays

For each of the files above I would like quotes for the period of
December 1944 - February 1945.
Any help you can offer in my getting copies these records will be
greatly appreciated.

Cordially,


Requester's Name

# NOTES:

## Introduction:

1. Fox, Geoffrey. "Who Are the Green Mountain Boys?" http://www.uvm.edu/~cemorse/Introducing%20VT%20Website/WHO%20ARE%20THE%20GREEN%20MOUNTAIN%20BOYS-web.html
2. Ibid.
3. *World War Two Honor List of Dead and Missing State of Vermont.* Washington, D.C.: War Department, 1946.
4. Ibid.
5. http://www.abmc.gov/publications/CemeteryBooklets/Henri-Chapelle_Booklet.pdf page 6
6. Ibid.
7. http://www.abmc.gov/cemeteries-memorials/europe/henri-chapelle-american-cemetery#.VOkSx2c5BMs
8. http://www.abmc.gov/home.php
9. http://www.abmc.gov/about-us/history
10. Ibid.
11. http://www.abmc.gov/home.php


## PVT Leroy Baker

1. "Vermont, Vital Records, 1760-1954," index and images, *FamilySearch* (https://familysearch.org/pal:/MM9.1.1/XFKL-1Y3: accessed 27 February 2013), Leroy Lester Baker, 1923.
2. Bressette, Cecilia. Personal interview. 25 March 2013.
3. Ibid.
4. "United States Census, 1930," index and images, *FamilySearch* (https://familysearch.org/pal:/MM9.1.1/XMZ9-G9H : accessed 27 February 2013), Le Roy L Baker in household of George E Baker, Pownal, Bennington, Vermont, United States; citing enumeration district (ED) 0018, sheet, family 318, NARA microfilm publication.
5. "United States Census, 1940," index and images, *FamilySearch* (https://familysearch.org/pal:/MM9.1.1/VYH4-J9L : accessed 27 February 2013), Leroy L Baker in household of George E Baker, Pownal Town, Bennington, Vermont, United States; citing

enumeration district (ED) 2-22, sheet 7A, family 133, NARA digital publication of T627, roll 4229.

6. Bressette, Cecilia. Personal interview. 25 March 2013.
7. Ibid.
8. Ibid.
9. Ibid.
10. Ibid.
11. Ibid.
12. Ibid.
13. Ibid.
14. Ibid.
15. Ibid.

## SGT Norman Bishop and PVT Lawrence Bishop

1. "Vermont, Vital Records, 1760-1954," index and images, *FamilySearch* (https://familysearch.org/pal:/MM9.1.1/XFKT-8PF : accessed 03 Dec 2012), Henry Eli Bishop in entry for Norman Edward Bishop, 1914.
2. Royer, Norine. Personal interview. 9 February 2013.
3. "Vermont, Vital Records, 1760-1954," index and images, *FamilySearch* (https://familysearch.org/pal:/MM9.1.1/XFKT-8PF : accessed 03 Dec 2012), Henry Eli Bishop in entry for Norman Edward Bishop, 1914.
4. "United States Census, 1920," index and images, *FamilySearch* (https://familysearch.org/pal:/MM9.1.1/MZYM-PDJ : accessed 03 Dec 2012), Norman E Bishop in household of Henry E Bishop, Morgan, Orleans, Vermont, United States; citing sheet, family 11, NARA microfilm publication T625, FHL microfilm 1821874.
5. Royer, Norine. Personal interview. 9 February 2013.
6. Ibid.
7. "United States Census, 1940," index and images, *FamilySearch* (https://familysearch.org/pal:/MM9.1.1/VYHX-N61 : accessed 03 Dec 2012), Lawrence H Bishop in household of Milton K Willey, Derby Town, Orleans, Vermont, United States; citing enumeration district (ED) 10-15, sheet 4A, family 60, NARA digital publication of T627, roll 4234.
8. Hall, Bev. Personal interview. 9 February 2013.

9. Royer, Norine. Personal interview. 9 February 2013.

10. "Vermont, Vital Records, 1760-1954," index and images, *FamilySearch* (https://familysearch.org/pal:/MM9.1.1/XF2X-Y6G : accessed 13 Dec 2012), Henry E Bishop, 1942.

11. "United States World War II Army Enlistment Records, 1938-1946," index, *FamilySearch* (https://familysearch.org/pal:/MM9.1.1/KMNB-S23 : accessed 03 Jan 2013), Lawrence H Bishop, 21 Dec 1943.

12. Royer, Norine. Personal interview. 9 February 2013.

13. Ibid.

14. Ibid.

15. Ibid.

16. *Newport Daily Express*. January 25, 1945.

17. Individual Deceased Personnel File.

18. Royer, Norine. Personal interview. 9 February 2013.

## PFC John Carleton

1. "Vermont, Vital Records, 1760-2003," index and images, *FamilySearch* (https://familysearch.org/pal:/MM9.1.1/KFTL-1DK : accessed 6 November 2014), John Elijah Carleton, Birth, 04 Nov 1922, Windham, Windham, Vermont, United States; derived from Vermont birth, marriage, and death indexes and images, 1909-2008, *Ancestry.com* (http://www.ancestry.com : 2010); citing Vital Records Office, Vermont Department of Health, Burlington; New England Historic Genealogical Society, Boston.

2. http://www.legacy.com/obituaries/rutlandherald/obituary.aspx?pid=169742061.

3. *Rutland Daily Herald*. March 23, 1945.

4. Ibid.

5. http://www.vermont-marble.com/.

6. "United States World War II Army Enlistment Records, 1938-1946," index, *FamilySearch* (https://familysearch.org/pal:/MM9.1.1/K8RS-XC1 : accessed 6 November 2014), John E Carleton, enlisted 29 Aug 1944, Rutland, Vermont, United States; citing "Electronic Army Serial Number Merged File, ca. 1938-1946," database, *The National Archives: Access to Archival Databases (AAD)* (http://aad.archives.gov : National Archives and Records Administration, 2002); NARA

ARC 126323, National Archives and Records Administration, Washington, D.C.
7. Individual Deceased Personnel File.
8. Ibid.

## PFC Claude Chapin

1. Chapin, Barbara. Personal interview. 8 February 2014.
2. Ibid.
3. Ibid.
4. Ibid.
5. Ibid.
6. Ibid.
7. Ibid.
8. Ibid.
9. Individual Deceased Personal File.
10. Chapin, Barbara. Personal interview. 8 February 2014.
11. Ibid.
12. Ibid.
13. Ibid.

## PFC Louis Connolly

1. Humphrey, Neil. E-mail interview. 22 May 2013.
2. Bills, Rosalee. Phone interview. 10 June 2013.
3. Bills, Rosalee. Letter interview. 22 September 2013.
4. Bills, Rosalee. Phone interview. 10 June 2013.
5. Bills, Rosalee. Letter interview. 22 September 2013.
6. Bills, Rosalee. Phone interview. 10 June 2013.
7. Bills, Rosalee. Letter interview. 22 September 2013.
8. Ibid.
9. Ibid.
10. Ibid.

## PVT Gerard Desroches

1. Guerin, Robert. E-mail interview. 15 November 2013.

## PVT James Durkee

1. "United States Census, 1940," index and images, *FamilySearch* (https://familysearch.org/pal:/MM9.1.1/VYH2-FHP : accessed 30 Nov 2013), James Durkee in household of Ralph Durkee, Norwich, Norwich Town, Windsor, Vermont, United States; citing enumeration district (ED) 14-21, sheet 5B, family 104, NARA digital publication of T627, roll 4240.
2. Durkee, Jackie. Personal interview. 30 November 2013.
3. Ibid.
4. Ibid.
5. Ibid.
6. Ibid.
7. Individual Deceased Personnel File.
8. Ibid.
9. Ibid.

## PVT Albert Gauthier

1. Gauthier, David and Lynn. E-mail interview. 29 March 2014.
2. http://www.datesinhistory.com/mar14.php.
3. Gauthier, David and Lynn. E-mail interview. 29 March 2014.
4. "United States World War II Army Enlistment Records, 1938-1946," index, *FamilySearch* (https://familysearch.org/pal:/MM9.1.1/ KMNB-Q79 : accessed 3 March 2014), Albert J Gauthier, enlisted 28 Dec 1943, Rutland, Vermont, United States; citing "Electronic Army Serial Number Merged File, ca. 1938-1946," database, *The National Archives: Access to Archival Databases (AAD)* (http://aad. archives.gov : National Archives and Records Administration, 2002); NARA ARC 126323, National Archives and Records Administration, Washington, D.C.
5. Ibid.
6. Gauthier, David and Lynn. E-mail interview. 29 March 2014.
7. Individual Deceased Personnel File.
8. *The Suburban List* October 26, 1944, Pg. 10, Column 1.
9. Gauthier, David and Lynn. E-mail interview. 29 March 2014.

## PFC Theodore Hall

1. "Vermont, Vital Records, 1760-2003," index and images, *FamilySearch* (https://familysearch.org/pal:/MM9.1.1/KFR5-1XZ : accessed 6 December 2013), Theodore Graham Hall and Helen Elizabeth Baker, Marriage, 07 Nov 1942, Springfield, Windsor, Vermont, United States; derived from Vermont birth, marriage, and death indexes and images, 1909-2008, *Ancestry.com* (http://www.ancestry.com : 2010); citing Vital Records Office, Vermont Department of Health, Burlington; New England Historic Genealogical Society, Boston.

2. "United States Census, 1940," index and images, *FamilySearch* (https://familysearch.org/pal:/MM9.1.1/KMMV-Q2V : accessed 6 November 2014), Theodore G Hall in household of Graham Hall, Jefferson Town, Lincoln, Maine, United States; citing enumeration district (ED) 8-16, sheet 1A, family 8, NARA digital publication of T627, roll 1483, NARA digital publication of T627, National Archives and Records Administration, Washington, D.C.

3. Enlistment Record.

4. "Vermont, Vital Records, 1760-2003," index and images, *FamilySearch* (https://familysearch.org/pal:/MM9.1.1/KFR5-1XZ : accessed 6 December 2013), Theodore Graham Hall and Helen Elizabeth Baker, Marriage, 07 Nov 1942, Springfield, Windsor, Vermont, United States; derived from Vermont birth, marriage, and death indexes and images, 1909-2008, *Ancestry.com* (http://www.ancestry.com : 2010); citing Vital Records Office, Vermont Department of Health, Burlington; New England Historic Genealogical Society, Boston

5. "United States World War II Army Enlistment Records, 1938-1946," index, *FamilySearch* (https://familysearch.org/pal:/MM9.1.1/KMNY-R5W : accessed 16 October 2014), Theodore G Hall, enlisted 09 Nov 1943, Portland, Maine, United States; citing "Electronic Army Serial Number Merged File, ca. 1938-1946," database, *The National Archives: Access to Archival Databases (AAD)* (http://aad.archives.gov : National Archives and Records Administration, 2002); NARA ARC 126323, National Archives and Records Administration, Washington, D.C.

6. Individual Deceased Personnel File.

7. Death notice. *Springfield Reporter*, May 17, 1945.

8. Baker, Gertrude. Letter interview. 29 December 2014.

9. Individual Deceased Personnel File.

10. Ibid.


# SSGT Arthur Jacobs

1. "Vermont, Vital Records, 1760-2003," index and images, *FamilySearch* (https://familysearch.org/pal:/MM9.1.1/KFYG-472 : accessed 20 February 2013), Arthur Loyde Jacobs, Birth, 09 Dec 1914, Barton, Orleans, Vermont, United States; derived from Vermont birth, marriage, and death indexes and images, 1909-2008, *Ancestry* (http://www.ancestry.com : 2010); citing Vital Records Office, Vermont Department of Health, Burlington; New England Historic Genealogical Society, Boston.

2. Jacobs, Arthur and Joyal, Florence. Personal interview. 20 January 2013.

3. Ibid.

4. Enlistment Record.

5. "Vermont, Vital Records, 1760-1954," index and images, *FamilySearch* (https://familysearch.org/pal:/MM9.1.1/2V32-RX7 : accessed 20 February 2013), Arthur Jacobs and Beatrice Todd, 01 Sep 1935, Marriage; State Capitol Building, Montpelier; FHL microfilm 2,032,735.

6. Ibid.

7. "Vermont, Vital Records, 1760-1954," index and images, *FamilySearch* (https://familysearch.org/pal:/MM9.1.1/2V3L-9ZK : accessed 20 February 2013), Arthur Lloyd Jacobs in entry for Malcolm Arthur Jacobs, 14 Apr 1936, Birth; State Capitol Building, Montpelier; FHL microfilm 2,032,735.

8. Jacobs, Arthur and Joyal, Florence. Personal interview. 20 January 2013.

9. "Vermont, Vital Records, 1760-1954," index and images, *FamilySearch* (https://familysearch.org/pal:/MM9.1.1/2V32-1ZH : accessed 20 February 2013), Arthur Lloyd Jacobs in entry for Edwin Roy Jacobs, 16 Feb 1938, Birth; State Capitol Building, Montpelier; FHL microfilm 2,032,735.

10. "United States Census, 1940," index and images, *FamilySearch* (https://familysearch.org/pal:/MM9.1.1/VYHX-Q2G : accessed 20 February 2013), Arthur Jacobs, Derby Line, Derby Town, Orleans, Vermont, United States; citing enumeration district (ED) 10-13, sheet 3A, family 56, NARA digital publication T627 (Washington, D.C.: National Archives and Records Administration, 2012), roll 4234.

11. "Vermont, Vital Records, 1760-1954," index and images, *FamilySearch* (https://familysearch.org/pal:/MM9.1.1/VNR7-N7W : accessed 20 February 2013), Arthur Lloyd Jacobs in entry for Melvin Ray Jacobs, 27 Jun 1942, Birth; State Capitol Building, Montpelier; FHL microfilm 1,991,390.

12. "Vermont, Vital Records, 1760-1954," index and images, *FamilySearch* (https://familysearch.org/pal:/MM9.1.1/VNR7-N38 : accessed 20 February 2013), Arthur Lloyd Jacobs in entry for Lorraine Fay Jacobs, 22 Aug 1943, Birth; State Capitol Building, Montpelier; FHL microfilm 1,991,390.

13. Individual Deceased Personnel File.

14. Enlistment Record.

15. "Vermont, Vital Records, 1760-1954," index and images, *FamilySearch* (https://familysearch.org/pal:/MM9.1.1/VNR7-RVH : accessed 20 February 2013), Arthur Jacobs in entry for Shiela Ann Jacobs, 30 Oct 1944, Death; State Capitol Building, Montpelier; FHL microfilm 1,991,390.

16. Jacobs, Arthur and Joyal, Florence. Personal interview. 20 January 2013.

17. "Vermont, Vital Records, 1760-2003," index and images, *FamilySearch* (https://familysearch.org/pal:/MM9.1.1/KFRY-CJD : accessed 20 February 2013), Arthur Jacobs in entry for Edwin Roy Jacobs, Death, 07 Feb 1954, Newport, Orleans, Vermont, United States; derived from Vermont birth, marriage, and death indexes and images, 1909-2008, *Ancestry* (http://www.ancestry.com : 2010); citing Vital Records Office, Vermont Department of Health, Burlington; New England Historic Genealogical Society, Boston.

18. Death notice. *Newport Daily Express.* 16 March 1945.

19. Jacobs, Arthur and Joyal, Florence. Personal interview. 20 January 2013.

## SGT Edward Jones Jr.

1. Individual Deceased Personnel File.
2. Ibid.
3. "United States World War II Army Enlistment Records, 1938-1946," index, *FamilySearch* (https://familysearch.org/pal:/MM9.1.1/K85P-31V : accessed 1 December 2014), Edward T Jr Jones, enlisted 14 Mar 1941, Rutland, Vermont, United States; citing "Electronic Army Serial Number Merged File, ca. 1938-1946," database, *The National Archives: Access to Archival Databases (AAD)* (http://aad.archives.gov : National Archives and Records Administration, 2002); NARA ARC 126323, National Archives and Records Administration, Washington, D.C.
4. Individual Deceased Personnel File.
5. Ibid.
6. Ibid.
7. Ibid.
8. Ibid.
9. Ibid.
10. Ibid.
11. Ibid.
12. Ibid.
13. Ibid.
14. http://web.timesunion.com/ASPStories/Story.asp?storyID=973479and newsdate=10/24/2010andBCCode=MBTAandTextPage=1
15. http://www.boston.com/yourtown/bos-ton/allston_brighton/articles/2010/09/24/remains_of_wwii_soldier_from_vt_to_be_buried/
16. http://www.boston.com/yourtown/norwood/articles/2010/04/29/remains_of_missing_arlington_native_killed_in_wwii_return_to_mass_for_burial/

## PVT Adelard Joyal and SSGT George Joyal

1. Joyal, George and Debra Viens. Letter interview. 14 September 2014.
2. "United States Census, 1930," index and images, *FamilySearch* (https://familysearch.org/pal:/MM9.1.1/XMZQ-8V3 : accessed 8 September 2014), George E Joyal in household of Charles E Joyal, Burlington, Chittenden, Vermont, United States; citing enumeration

district (ED) 0025, sheet 17B, family 278, line 51, NARA microfilm publication T626 (Washington D.C.: National Archives and Records Administration, 2002), roll 2427; FHL microfilm 2,342,161.

3. Joyal, George and Debra Viens. Letter interview. 14 September 2014.

4. "United States World War II Army Enlistment Records, 1938-1946," index, *FamilySearch* (https://familysearch.org/pal:/MM9.1.1/K85R-8T8 : accessed 12 July 2014), Adelard Joyal, enlisted 25 Jun 1942, Rutland, Vermont, United States; citing "Electronic Army Serial Number Merged File, ca. 1938-1946," database, *The National Archives: Access to Archival Databases (AAD)* (http://aad.archives.gov : National Archives and Records Administration, 2002); NARA NAID 126323, National Archives and Records Administration, Washington, D.C.

5. Joyal, George and Debra Viens. Letter interview. 14 September 2014.

6. "Vermont, Vital Records, 1760-2003," index and images, *FamilySearch* (https://familysearch.org/pal:/MM9.1.1/KFY6-XFL : accessed 12 August 2014), George Emile Joyal and Constance Mable Gorman, Marriage, 30 Aug 1941, Burlington, Chittenden, Vermont, United States; derived from Vermont birth, marriage, and death indexes and images, 1909-2008, *Ancestry* (http://www.ancestry.com : 2010); citing Vital Records Office, Vermont Department of Health, Burlington; New England Historic Genealogical Society, Boston.

7. Joyal, George. E-mail interview. 30 September 2014.

8. "United States World War II Army Enlistment Records, 1938-1946," index, *FamilySearch* (https://familysearch.org/pal:/MM9.1.1/KMNR-CYX : accessed 12 August 2014), George E Joyal, enlisted 22 Dec 1942, Ft Devens, Massachusetts, United States; citing "Electronic Army Serial Number Merged File, ca. 1938-1946," database, *The National Archives: Access to Archival Databases (AAD)* (http://aad.archives.gov : National Archives and Records Administration, 2002); NARA NAID 126323, National Archives and Records Administration, Washington, D.C.

9. Individual Deceased Personnel File.

10. Ibid.

11. Joyal, George and Debra Viens. Letter interview. 14 September 2014.

12. Joyal, George. E-mail interview. 30 September 2014.

13. Ibid.

# PFC Howard Lapan

1. "Vermont, Vital Records, 1760-1954," index and images, *FamilySearch* (https://familysearch.org/pal:/MM9.1.1/2V31-PK5 : accessed 10 September 2014), Howard Douglas Lapan, 05 May 1923, Birth; State Capitol Building, Montpelier; FHL microfilm 2,033,343.

2. "United States Census, 1930," index and images, *FamilySearch* (https://familysearch.org/pal:/MM9.1.1/XMZW-5SL : accessed 6 October 2014), Howard D Lapan in household of Ernest Lapan, Johnson, Lamoille, Vermont, United States; citing enumeration district (ED) 0010, sheet 5B, family 108, line 61, film number 2429, NARA microfilm publication T626, (Washington D.C.: National Archives and Records Administration, 2002); FHL microfilm 2,342,163.

3. "United States World War II Army Enlistment Records, 1938-1946," index, *FamilySearch* (https://familysearch.org/pal:/MM9.1.1/K8R3-GVW : accessed 6 October 2014), Howard D Lapan, enlisted 12 Jun 1944, Ft Devens, Massachusetts, United States; citing "Electronic Army Serial Number Merged File, ca. 1938-1946," database, *The National Archives: Access to Archival Databases (AAD)* (http://aad.archives.gov : National Archives and Records Administration, 2002); NARA ARC 126323, National Archives and Records Administration, Washington, D.C.

4. "United States Census, 1910," index and images, *FamilySearch* (https://familysearch.org/pal:/MM9.1.1/MPF4-BCQ : accessed 12 January 2014), Eliza M Patch in household of Charles M Patch, Johnson, Lamoille, Vermont, United States; citing enumeration district (ED) 129, sheet 14A, family 351, NARA microfilm publication T624, National Archives and Records Administration, Washington, D.C.; FHL microfilm 1,375,625.

5. "Vermont, Vital Records, 1760-1954," index and images, *FamilySearch* (https://familysearch.org/pal:/MM9.1.1/2V31-2XG : accessed 1 December 2014), Ernest Lapan, 09 Jan 1936, Death; State Capitol Building, Montpelier; FHL microfilm 2,033,343.

6. Individual Deceased Personnel File.

7. Ibid.

8. Death notice. *News and Citizen*, April 12, 1945.

## CPL Maurice Metivier

1. "Vermont, Vital Records, 1760-1954," index and images, *FamilySearch* (https://familysearch.org/pal:/MM9.1.1/XFX3-ZZQ : accessed 7 October 2014), Morris George Metivier, 17 Jun 1908, Birth; State Capitol Building, Montpelier; FHL microfilm 540,121.

2. "United States Census, 1930," index and images, *FamilySearch* (https://familysearch.org/pal:/MM9.1.1/XMZQ-21R : accessed 7 October 2014), Maurice Metivier in household of George A Metivier, Winooski, Chittenden, Vermont, United States; citing enumeration district (ED) 0046, sheet 4B, family 83, line 57, film number 2428, NARA microfilm publication T626, (Washington D.C.: National Archives and Records Administration, 2002); FHL microfilm 2,342,162.

3. "United States World War II Army Enlistment Records, 1938-1946," index, *FamilySearch* (https://familysearch.org/pal:/MM9.1.1/K8L6-2Z2 : accessed 7 October 2014), Maurice G Metivier, enlisted 29 Oct 1940, Ft Ethan Allen, Vermont, United States; citing "Electronic Army Serial Number Merged File, ca. 1938-1946," database, *The National Archives: Access to Archival Databases (AAD)* (http://aad.archives.gov : National Archives and Records Administration, 2002); NARA ARC 126323, National Archives and Records Administration, Washington, D.C.

4. "Vermont, Vital Records, 1760-1954," index and images, *FamilySearch* (https://familysearch.org/pal:/MM9.1.1/2VQ8-3W7 : accessed 5 October 2014), Wanda Ann Metivier, 18 Aug 1941, Birth; State Capitol Building, Montpelier; FHL microfilm 2,050,525.

5. Individual Deceased Personnel File.

6. Death Notice. *Burlington Free Press*. March 19, 1945.

7. Eggleston, Gerry. Letter interview. 9 November 2014.

## PFC Harold Mitchell

1. "Vermont, Vital Records, 1760-1954," index and images, *FamilySearch* (https://familysearch.org/pal:/MM9.1.1/VNRK-MVC : accessed 15 November 2014), Harold Kenneth Mitchell and Beulah Atrude Mumley, 16 Sep 1944, Marriage; State Capitol Building, Montpelier; FHL microfilm 2,022,656.

2. "United States Census, 1930," index and images, *FamilySearch* (https://familysearch.org/pal:/MM9.1.1/XMZS-9H8 : accessed 15 November 2014), Harold K Mitchell in household of William W Mitchell, Alburg, Grand Isle, Vermont, United States; citing enumeration district (ED) 0001, sheet 6A, family 128, line 37, film number 2426, NARA microfilm publication T626, (Washington D.C.: National Archives and Records Administration, 2002); FHL microfilm 2,342,160.

3. Jr. Mitchell, Harold. Letter interview. 9 November 2014.

4. Enlistment Record.

5. Missing in Action notice. *Burlington Free Press*. 22 January 1945.

6. Individual Deceased Personnel File.

7. Ibid.

8. "Vermont, Vital Records, 1760-1954," index and images, *FamilySearch* (https://familysearch.org/pal:/MM9.1.1/VNRK-MV8 : accessed 10 September 2014), Harold K Mitchell in entry for Harold Kenneth Mitchell, 08 Aug 1945, Birth; State Capitol Building, Montpelier; FHL microfilm 2,022,656.

9. Jr. Mitchell, Harold. Letter interview. 9 November 2014.

10. Ibid.

11. Ibid.

## Tec 5 Raymond Muir

1. http://genforum.genealogy.com/wwii/messages/2249.html.

2. http://www.fieldsofhonor-database.com/index.php/ american-war-cemetery-henri-chapelle-m/48704-muir-raymond-h.

3. http://genforum.genealogy.com/wwii/messages/2249.html.

4. Individual Deceased Personnel File.

5. Ibid.

## PVT Harvey Colton Oliver

1. Individual Deceased Personnel File.

2. "Vermont, Vital Records, 1760-1954," index and images, *FamilySearch* (https://familysearch.org/pal:/MM9.1.1/XFG8-ZD6 : accessed 15 September 2014), Charles Oliver and Olive Morey Colton, 21 Jul 1920, Marriage; State Capitol Building, Montpelier; FHL microfilm 1,984,645.

3. "United States Census, 1930," index and images, *FamilySearch* (https://familysearch.org/pal:/MM9.1.1/XMP5-S1J : accessed 10 September 2014), Harvey C Oliver in household of Charles Oliver, Manchester, Hartford, Connecticut, United States; citing enumeration district (ED) 0148, sheet 9B, family 224, line 79, film number 267, NARA microfilm publication T626, (Washington D.C.: National Archives and Records Administration, 2002); FHL microfilm 2,340,002.

4. "United States Census, 1940," index and images, *FamilySearch* (https://familysearch.org/pal:/MM9.1.1/VYHX-YZ5 : accessed 10 September 2014), Harvey C Oliver in household of Charles Oliver, Brandon Town, Rutland, Vermont, United States; citing enumeration district (ED) 11-2, sheet 11A, family 222, NARA digital publication of T627, roll 4235, NARA digital publication of T627, National Archives and Records Administration, Washington, D.C.

5. "United States World War II Army Enlistment Records, 1938-1946," index, *FamilySearch* (https://familysearch.org/pal:/MM9.1.1/K8R9-SGV : accessed 5 October 2014), Y Zveq C Olivvr, enlisted 29 Sep 1943, Rutland, Vermont, United States; citing "Electronic Army Serial Number Merged File, ca. 1938-1946," database, *The National Archives: Access to Archival Databases (AAD)* (http://aad.archives.gov : National Archives and Records Administration, 2002); NARA ARC 126323, National Archives and Records Administration, Washington, D.C.

6. Individual Deceased Personnel File.

7. http://archive.org/stream/townundercliffhi00robi/townundercliffhi-00robi_djvu.txt

8. Individual Deceased Personnel File.

9. Death notice. *Rutland Daily Herald*. January 16, 1945.

## PVT Maurice Ploof

1. Individual Deceased Personnel File.

2. "United States Census, 1930," index and images, *FamilySearch* (https://familysearch.org/pal:/MM9.1.1/XMZW-Z9X : accessed 10 August 2014), Maurice M Ploof in household of Trifley R Ploof, Sheldon, Franklin, Vermont, United States; citing enumeration district (ED) 0023, sheet 2A, family 17, line 5, film number 2428,

NARA microfilm publication T626, (Washington D.C.: National Archives and Records Administration, 2002); FHL microfilm 2,342,162.

3. "United States Census, 1940," index and images, *FamilySearch* (https://familysearch.org/pal:/MM9.1.1/VYHD-C44 : accessed 10 August 2014), Maurice Plouffe in household of Treffle Plouffe, Ward 6, Saint Albans, St. Albans City, Franklin, Vermont, United States; citing enumeration district (ED) 6-29, sheet 6B, family 128, NARA digital publication of T627, roll 4232, NARA digital publication of T627, National Archives and Records Administration, Washington, D.C.

4. Death notice. *St. Albans Daily Messenger*. January 27, 1945.

### CAPT Richard Prentiss

1. http://www.findagrave.com/cgi-bin/fg.cgi?page=gr&GRid=56284707.
2. http://www.416th.com/668th_history_usaf_afhra_transcription.pdf.
3. Ibid.
4. http://www.findagrave.com/cgi-bin/fg.cgi?page=gr&GRid=56284707.
5. http://www.rgprucha.com/prucha_brennan/lou_wwii/lou_wwii_combat_mission_176.htm.
6. http://www.rgprucha.com/prucha_brennan/lou_wwii/lou_wwii_combat_mission_176.htm.
7. http://www.rgprucha.com/prucha_brennan/lou_wwii/lou_wwii_combat_mission_176.htm.

### PFC Royal Rogers

1. "Vermont, Vital Records, 1760-2003," index and images, *FamilySearch* (https://familysearch.org/pal:/MM9.1.1/KNSJ-BPW : accessed 12 January 2014), Royal Rufus Rogers, Birth, 11 Sep 1918, Berkshire, Franklin, Vermont, United States; derived from Vermont birth, marriage, and death indexes and images, 1909-2008, *Ancestry* (http://www.ancestry.com : 2010); citing Vital Records Office, Vermont Department of Health, Burlington; New England Historic Genealogical Society, Boston.

2. Rogers. Peter. E-mail interview. 16 January 2014.
3. Ibid.
4. Ibid.

5. Ibid.

6. Individual Deceased Personnel File

7. "United States Census, 1910," index and images, *FamilySearch* (https://familysearch.org/pal:/MM9.1.1/MPF4-BCQ : accessed 12 January 2014), Eliza M Patch in household of Charles M Patch, Johnson, Lamoille, Vermont, United States; citing enumeration district (ED) 129, sheet 14A, family 351, NARA microfilm publication T624, National Archives and Records Administration, Washington, D.C.; FHL microfilm 1,375,625.

8. "Vermont, Vital Records, 1760-1954," index and images, *FamilySearch* (https://familysearch.org/pal:/MM9.1.1/VNRP-6YK : accessed 12 January 2014), Royal R Rogers and Shirley C Patch, 16 Jul 1942, Marriage; State Capitol Building, Montpelier; FHL microfilm 2,023,182.

9. "Vermont, Vital Records, 1760-1954," index and images, *FamilySearch* (https://familysearch.org/pal:/MM9.1.1/2V36-G4L : accessed 12 January 2014), Shirley Christina Patch in entry for Larry William Rogers, 05 Feb 1943, Birth; State Capitol Building, Montpelier; FHL microfilm 2,023,992.

10. Individual Deceased Personnel File.

11. Rogers, Peter. E-mail interview. 16 January 2014.

12. Individual Deceased Personnel File.

13. Ibid.

14. Ibid.

15. Ibid.

16. "Vermont, Vital Records, 1760-2003," index and images, *FamilySearch* (https://familysearch.org/pal:/MM9.1.1/KFPD-D8H : accessed 12 January 2014), Larry William Rogers, Death, 14 Nov 2002, Burlington, Chittenden, Vermont, United States; derived from Vermont birth, marriage, and death indexes and images, 1909-2008, *Ancestry* (http://www.ancestry.com : 2010); citing Vital Records Office, Vermont Department of Health, Burlington; New England Historic Genealogical Society, Boston.

### PVT Durward Rollins

1. "Vermont, Vital Records, 1760-1954," index and images, *FamilySearch* (https://familysearch.org/pal:/MM9.1.1/XF6J-RZR :

accessed 13 September 2014), Durward Warner Rollins, 19 Jun 1908, Birth; State Capitol Building, Montpelier; FHL microfilm 540,139.

2. "Vermont, Vital Records, 1760-1954," index and images, *FamilySearch* (https://familysearch.org/pal:/MM9.1.1/XF6J-RZR : accessed 13 September 2014), Durward Warner Rollins, 19 Jun 1908, Birth; State Capitol Building, Montpelier; FHL microfilm 540,139.

3. "United States Census, 1910," index and images, *FamilySearch* (https://familysearch.org/pal:/MM9.1.1/MPFV-DT1 : accessed 1 October 2014), Durward W Rollins in household of Claude M Rollins, Hardwick, Caledonia, Vermont, United States; citing enumeration district (ED) 44, sheet 16A, family 358, NARA microfilm publication T624, National Archives and Records Administration, Washington, D.C.; FHL microfilm 1,375,626.

4. "United States World War II Army Enlistment Records, 1938-1946," index, *FamilySearch* (https://familysearch.org/pal:/MM9.1.1/K8RS-8N7 : accessed 1 October 2014), Durward W Rollins, enlisted 15 Nov 1943, Rutland, Vermont, United States; citing "Electronic Army Serial Number Merged File, ca. 1938-1946," database, *The National Archives: Access to Archival Databases (AAD)* (http://aad.archives. gov : National Archives and Records Administration, 2002); NARA NAID 126323, National Archives and Records Administration, Washington, D.C.

5. "Vermont, Vital Records, 1760-1954," index and images, *FamilySearch* (https://familysearch.org/pal:/MM9.1.1/2V3B-WTT : accessed 1 October 2014), Durward Warner Rollins and Irene Belle Kingsley, 23 Oct 1935, Marriage; State Capitol Building, Montpelier; FHL microfilm 2,033,200.

6. "Vermont, Vital Records, 1760-1954," index and images, *FamilySearch* (https://familysearch.org/pal:/MM9.1.1/2V36-KWS : accessed 1 October 2014), Durward Warner Rollins in entry for Rhoda Irene Rollins, 02 Jun 1944, Birth; State Capitol Building, Montpelier; FHL microfilm 2,023,992.

7. Individual Deceased Personnel File.
8. Ibid.
9. Ibid.
10. Death notice. *Burlington Free Press*. March 10, 1945.

## PVT Thomas Sorrell

1. Sorrell, James. E-mail interview. 31 July 2014.
2. Individual Deceased Personnel File.
3. Ibid.
4. Ibid.
5. Ibid.
6. Ibid.
7. Ibid.
8. Ibid.
9. Ibid.
10. Ibid.
11. Ibid.
12. Siple, Helen. Letter interview. 25 July 2014.
13. Sorrell, James. E-mail interview. 25 August 2014.
14. Siple, Helen. Letter interview. 25 July 2014.
15. Ibid.
16. Ibid.
17. Ibid.
18. Sorrell, James. E-mail interview. 25 August 2014.
19. Sorrell, James. E-mail interview. 7 December 2014.
20. Sorrell, James. E-mail interview. 19 December 2014.

## PVT Logan Warner

1. "Vermont, Vital Records, 1760-1954," index and images,
   *FamilySearch* (https://familysearch.org/pal:/MM9.1.1/2V77-8SV :
   accessed 10 October 2014), Logan Edwin Warner, 28 Jul 1922, Birth;
   State Capitol Building, Montpelier; FHL microfilm 2,073,260.
2. Gruber, Natalie. Letter interview. 7 October 2014.
3. Ibid.
4. Ibid.
5. Ibid.
6. Individual Deceased Personnel File.
7. Gruber, Natalie. Letter interview. 7 October 2014.
8. Ibid.
9. Individual Deceased Personnel File.
10. Death notice. *Springfield Reporter*. 1 February 1945.
11. Gruber, Natalie. Letter interview. 7 October 2014.

## PFC Garth Whittier

1. Holt, Shirley and Catherine McKenney. Letter interview. 25 September 2014.
2. Ibid.
3. Ibid.
4. Ibid.
5. Individual Deceased Personnel File.
6. Ibid.
7. Ibid.